Casemate Sh

# TANKS

## A CENTURY OF TANK WARFARE

Oscar Gilbert and Romain Cansière

## CASEMATE
*Oxford & Philadelphia*

To our friends and associates in the
American and French tank communities,
active duty and retired.

Published in Great Britain and
the United States of America in 2017 by
CASEMATE PUBLISHERS
The Old Music Hall, 106–108 Cowley Road, Oxford OX4 1JE, UK and
1950 Lawrence Road, Havertown, PA 19083, USA

© Casemate Publishers 2017

Paperback Edition: ISBN 978-1-61200-490-7
Digital Edition: ISBN 978-1-61200-491-4

A CIP record for this book is available from the British Library

Printed in the Czech Republic by FINIDR, s.r.o.

For a complete list of Casemate titles, please contact:

CASEMATE PUBLISHERS (UK)
Telephone (01865) 241249
Email: casemate-uk@casematepublishers.co.uk
www.casematepublishers.co.uk

CASEMATE PUBLISHERS (US)
Telephone (610) 853-9131
Fax (610) 853-9146
Email: casemate@casematepublishers.com
www.casematepublishers.com

# CONTENTS

# TANK COMPONENT TERMINOLOGY
## AMERICAN M60A1 RISE

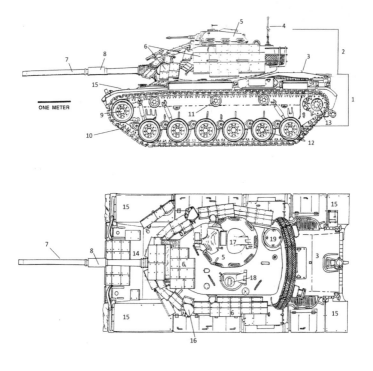

ONE METER

1. Hull
2. Turret
3. Engine deck
4. Radio antenna
5. Commander's cupola
6. Reactive armor blocks
7. Main gun tube
8. Bore evacuator

9. Idler wheel
10. Track
11. Track return roller
12. Road wheel
13. Drive sprocket
14. Glacis plate
15. Fender
16. Smoke grenade discharger

17. Commander's hatch
18. Loader's hatch
19. Ventilator

*Driver's hatch and main gun mantlet not visible*

# INTRODUCTION

*Military doctrine is what we believe about the best way to conduct military affairs.*

Dennis Drew and Don Snow, *Military Doctrine*

THIS SHORT HISTORY WILL EXPLORE THE evolution and historical use of the tank, but not in the usual way. There will be little emphasis on the technical aspects—engine horsepower, armor thickness, weapons caliber and penetration—as those data are available from innumerable books and websites. Instead we will delve into the history of how developmental decisions were made, and the evolving doctrine for the use of the tank.

Understanding doctrine is fundamental in that it controls the design of weapons systems like the tank. The interaction of doctrine and design concept is seen repeatedly, from the French and German internal squabbles between advocates of a few infantry tanks versus swarms of light tanks in the 1930s, through the diametrically opposed Soviet versus American/Western European doctrines of numerous expendable tanks (and crews) versus limited numbers of sophisticated tanks with increased crew survivability, respectively, in the late 20th century.

Sound doctrine will often atone for technical and numerical inferiority, but not vice versa. Examples are the rapid defeat of the French Army and British Expeditionary Force in 1940 by numerically and technically inferior German forces, and the humiliating defeats suffered by numerically superior Arab armies at the hands of the Israelis.

Doctrine outlives its creators. Doctrines developed by the now defunct Nazi Germany and Soviet Union continue to impact today's world. Doctrine affects the morale of tank crewmen, and like infantry the morale and training of tank crews fundamentally affects battlefield success. There are surprisingly many examples of incidents where tank crews retreated in disarray, or even abandoned their vehicles and fled on foot.

But first let's clear away the false romanticism that has attached itself to tank warfare. The efforts of propagandists to the contrary, tank crewmen are painfully aware that they are not the heirs to the romanticism of knightly combat.

The tank, from its very inception until today, has remained fundamentally an infantry support weapon. The tank was conceived as a way to end the bloody stalemate of the Western Front in World War I. By World War II the overwhelming majority of tanks still served in the infantry support role, but the realization grew that the best weapon to keep the enemy's tanks off

**Doctrine** is best defined as an overarching set of fundamental principles and a guide to action—rather than fixed rules—to allow for initiative. Doctrine provides a common language and frame of reference, helps standardize operations, and facilitates readiness. It links theory with actual practice, and provides an authoritative frame of reference on how a nation's military forces conduct operations.

your infantry was your own tank. So even tank-on-tank combat was simply an extension of the tank's infantry support role.

Late in World War II the image of tank warfare was hijacked. Eager to boost flagging national morale, Nazi propagandists seized upon the idea of the tank ace. Tank commanders like Michael Wittmann and Otto Carius became celebrities, with the Nazi press emphasizing battlefield "scores" and publishing idealized portraits of Germany's new knights. Yet even in World War II Germany the tank ace did not gain traction, and in fact most of the romance of the tank ace is a late 20th-century fabrication. Successful Allied tank commanders like American Sergeant Lafayette Poole never became vaunted heroes. To a man, veteran tank crewmen (some of whom would qualify as "tank aces") interviewed by the authors scoff at the idea. As several commented, it was just a brutal job to be done.

## Armored Vehicles in History

The oldest ancestor of the tank was the war chariot. Chariots provided mobility and striking power, but no practical armored protection, particularly for the equine propulsion system. Horsepower limitations placed severe restrictions on how heavily the vehicle might be armored and still retain its primary asset, mobility. The Egyptian solution, a light wicker body with springs to absorb shock, proved the best design of the ancient world, combining high speed, maneuverability, and stability that increased the striking power of the archer.

The first truly "modern" armored fighting vehicles were the battle-wagons (Czech *vozová hradba*) used by the Bohemian Hussites, a dissenting nationalist and religious sect. After Huss was burned at the stake in 1415, his followers fought a war from 1420 until 1434 against the Holy Roman Empire and the kingdom of Hungary. Hussite military leader John Zizka was centuries ahead of his time in designing practical fighting vehicles, formulating a doctrine for their use, and even inventing the concept of mobile field artillery. His battle-wagons were heavy agricultural wagons, fitted with wooden drop-sides to close off the area between the wheels, and built up sides to protect the occupants. Each carried between four and eight crossbowmen and a pair of men with primitive muskets for striking power, an equal number of pikemen for defense, and two drivers. A second type carried swivel-mounted "snakes"—small cannon.

Zizka's battle doctrine totally baffled enemy leaders, and he never lost a battle. The battle-wagons would move into a tactically advantageous position, form a circular laager with the vulnerable horses inside, and fortify by deploying the wooden panels. This inevitably goaded an enemy into an attack, which was inevitably repulsed by archers and snakes inside the laager. Zizka's troops were trained to quickly unleash his own cavalry from inside the laager, hitch the horses to the wagons, and commence a pursuit phase. Crossbowmen firing from inside the moving wagons worked considerable slaughter as they chased down fleeing enemy infantry.

Contrary to common knowledge, Leonardo DaVinci did not invent the idea of the tank, but in 1487 he did design a vehicle that might have been remotely practical. His design foundered on the usual problem—an effective propulsion/mobility system—and like most of his fanciful devices it was never built. Leonardo's design relied upon a crew of eight hand-cranking a system of wooden gears to drive wooden wheels positioned underneath the monstrously heavy vehicle. In concept it would be moved up to the enemy infantry line where it would serve as a sort of mobile fortress and firepower base, and Leonardo

 A **laager** (from the South African Boer language) is an impromptu fort made by circling vehicles, as in the old American cowboy movies.

was particularly insistent that it must be supported by infantry. Given the probable weight, moving a short distance even on a flat, modern paved surface would have been quite impractical.

For all this, the modern armored fighting vehicle really traces many of its key aspects back to the shipbuilder's craft. The first vessels to combine the three basic assets of armored vehicles—mobility, armored protection, and striking power—were sailing ships.

The first true modern armored warship was the CSS *Virginia*, first employed on February 17, 1862. At first the *Virginia* had it all its own way until the appearance of the Union armored ship USS *Monitor*. The *Monitor*, designed by John Ericsson, introduced a unique feature that would revolutionize both naval and land warfare—the rotating turret. On March 9, 1862, the two ships fought to a draw in the battle of Hampton Roads. The naval architects had solved the problem of mobility with the steam engine, but limited internal space for fuel, and above all the enormous amount of energy required to move over rough surfaces meant that the land ironclad remained a fantasy. Inventors were particularly active in the design of steam-powered armored land combat vehicles, but the prize had to go to Kaiser Wilhelm I: his contribution was a fantastic five-level, steam-powered monstrosity mounting no fewer than 100 cannon. The design closely resembled a heavily armed hotel building.

Two late 19th-century inventions revolutionized the idea of a land combat vehicle: the internal combustion engine, and the track. As early as the 1770s inventors strove to solve the problem of heavy vehicles bogging down in soft ground by distributing the weight on tracks, and for over a century inventors in several nations struggled with the idea of a practical track system. By the beginning of the 20th century, steam-powered tracked vehicles were in widespread use by the farming and timber-cutting industries. Despite several tests, the British Royal Artillery declined to adopt steam tractors. (It was during one of these tests that an anonymous British Tommy coined the name "caterpillar" for the peculiar track system.) It was the combination of the track with

Karl Benz's internal combustion engine that changed everything. The first truly practical artillery tractor was the American-made Holt, used by the British and Austro-Hungarian armies.

The very first known design for a true modern tracked and armored fighting vehicle was something that would reappear as a World War II German "innovation"—the assault gun. In 1903, a French captain, Léon René Levavasseur, proposed the Projet de Canon Autopulsier, an armored box mounted on caterpillar tracks, with a cannon mounted to fire out through the front plate. In late 1908, the project was terminated by the Comité Général d'Artillerie. It is not clear whether future French tank advocate General Jean-Baptiste Eugène Estienne was ever aware of the project.

The first modern armored vehicles came out of the global fascination with the new automobiles. The initial designs were as impractical as the cars they were based upon, but the 1906 French Charron-Giradot et Voigt armored car was quickly followed by a German Daimler armored car. Both incorporated Ericsson's rotating turret. Within a few years inventors all over the world were designing armored cars, with varying degrees of success.

Another major innovation was the machine gun. The first practical belt-fed, fully automatic machine gun was Hiram Maxim's 1883 gun. Such a light, relatively compact weapon was ideal for use in the close confines of a vehicle, and various machine-gun designs soon equipped most armored cars. The Italians used Bianchi armored cars to good effect around Tripoli, Libya in the 1911 Italo-Turkish War, and again in the Balkans (1912). Their successes had absolutely no effect on the tradition-bound military leadership of other European countries. Most were content with deploying masses of infantry and cavalry, lacked knowledgeable technical staffs, and were not at all interested in relatively untested "toys."

The machine gun's fiendish companion was another American innovation that would revolutionize 20th-century warfare and spur development of the tank: barbed wire. First used as a military obstacle in the 1904–05 Russo-Japanese War, the lessons of its effectiveness were also ignored.

Military leaders of European countries, fixated upon wars of colonial conquest, failed to absorb basic lessons from the American Civil War. Many European armies sent observers, but since the United States was regarded as a second- or third-rate power, they felt there were few lessons to be learned. They ignored the fact that improved rifles and artillery imposed hideous casualties on traditional massed frontal attacks. More inexplicable, European leaders ignored the lessons of their own colonial wars, in which massed firepower slaughtered "primitive" warriors in vast numbers.

German success in the 1870 Franco-Prussian War also taught few lessons, and instilled in both sides the idea that man would always prevail against mere materiel. That heavy casualties incurred when the Prussians encountered powerful French fortifications around Paris were ignored. Similarly, the lessons of the Russo-Japanese War, which bogged down into positional warfare because of massive firepower and barbed wire, were ignored. The European nations had modestly labeled themselves "First Class Powers," and resolutely ignored the lessons to be learned from squabbles among the "Second Class Powers."

By 1914 all the factors that would lead to the modern armored fighting vehicle—the tank—were in place. But while the leaders of the Great Power armies—most of whom were cavalrymen—continued to ignore creeping mechanization, it was increasingly felt in the less hidebound artillery. Experiments with tractors were in full swing, but as yet no one realized the primacy that mobile field artillery would soon assume.

| | |
|---|---|
| **1429–34** | John Zizka of Bohemia builds the first practical armored fighting vehicles. |
| **1487** | Leonardo DaVinci designs fanciful armored vehicle. |
| **1903** | French Captain Léon René Levavasseur designs a tracked, self-propelled armored cannon. |
| **1914** | British Lieutenant Colonel Ernest D. Swinton conceives the idea of the tank. |
| **1915** | May: Battling bureaucracies within the French government design two heavy tanks. General Jean-Baptiste Eugène Estienne develops more strategic use for tanks. |
| **1916** | September: The British first use tanks in battle. |
| | November: The French adopt the Renault faible tonnage (FT) light tank. |
| **1918** | April: First tank-on-tank battle: three British heavy tanks engage a German A7V. |
| **1918–39** | By war's end Britain, America, and France have all devised doctrines for armor. Over next two decades, tanks used in local wars, but in general tank design and doctrine stagnates. |
| **1929** | Japan introduces the I-Go heavy tank. |
| **1934** | The Soviets form two mechanized divisions and made tanks organic to every infantry division as part of their "deep battle" doctrine. |
| **1936–38** | Soviet tank corps disbanded in Stalinist purges. Germany introduces the Panzer IA, a thinly armored and poorly armed light tank. |
| **1936–39** | Spanish Civil War serves as a testing ground for German and Soviet weaponry. |
| **1939** | May: Soviet armored forces crush the Japanese Kwantung Army at Khalkhin Gol. |
| | September: Nazi and Soviet invasion crushes Poland. Western analysts draw false conclusions about German weapons and doctrine. |
| **1940** | Superior German doctrine results in the rapid subjugation of France. |
| **1940–43** | North Africa campaigns. Contemporary analysts place much of the blame for British and American defeats on flawed doctrine. |

| **1941–42** | The Japanese advance swiftly in the Pacific and East Asia, defeating numerically superior Allied tank forces. |
| **1943** | July: Kursk, the biggest armored clash in history. |
| | November: Gilbert Islands campaign marks major turning point in American tank doctrine. |
| **1944** | June–August: Operation *Bagration*, the Soviets implement their tank-based deep battle doctrine, destroying three German field armies. |
| | June: Invasion of Normandy, Allied armor has secondary role until late July, after which fast-moving armored forces destroy much of the Wehrmacht in France. |
| | December: Hitler squanders most of remaining German armored reserves in the west in the ill-advised Ardennes offensive. |
| **1947–91** | The Cold War. Tank design and doctrine of both sides grows increasingly sophisticated; introduction of the Main Battle Tank concept. |
| **1950–53** | Korean War. After a brief period of fluid warfare, tanks revert to infantry support role. |
| **1954** | June: Destruction of the French Groupement Mobile No. 100 armored force in Indochina. |
| **1965–75** | Vietnam War. American and Australian tanks provide important infantry support. The North Vietnamese make little use of tanks until the final stages of the war. |
| **1979** | Sino-Vietnamese War: China makes limited use of tanks, but it spurs the future development of a Chinese tank industry. |
| **1979–89** | Soviet invasion of Afghanistan results in defeat as strong Soviet armored forces unsuited to a guerrilla war. |
| **1990–** | Tanks play a major role in the doctrine of rapid dominance ("shock and awe") in two wars in Iraq, and have increasingly played an infantry support role in 21st-century counterinsurgencies. |
| **1994–96** | Chechnya declares independence. Invading Russian armor suffers humiliating defeat. |

# CHAPTER 1

# THE GREAT WAR OF 1914–18 AND THE BIRTH OF THE TANK

*Tanks in common with all other auxiliary arms are but means of aiding infantry, on whom the fate of battle forever rests, to drive their bayonets into the bellies of the enemy.*

Colonel George S. Patton, 1918

THE BRITISH WERE THE FIRST TO develop a functioning tank, but it was an idea whose time had come, and the French were close behind. All designs were directed toward solution of the strictly tactical problem of breaching German barbed-wire defenses, but the tank doctrines of the two major Allied powers—France and England—diverged as the result of design innovations. A third Allied power, the United States, proposed a sound doctrine based on a combined-arms force built around tanks, but it entered the war too late and the concept would not come to fruition for two decades.

In the East, Imperial Russian attempts to design a functional combat vehicle failed through shortcomings of industrial technology, although designs ranged from the innovative to the bizarre. Of the Central Powers only Germany developed a functional tank, but their General Staff ignored tanks until it was too late. Their single serviceable tank design was poorly conceived, and coherent doctrine non-existent.

By October 1914, the fighting on the Western Front had stalled. British Lieutenant Colonel Ernest D. Swinton conceived the idea of an armored and armed vehicle based on the American Holt tractor that a friend had described as "a Yankee tractor which could climb like the devil." Swinton's concept was given the cold shoulder by the War Office, but caught the attention of the ambitious First Lord of the Admiralty, Winston Churchill. Churchill's fleet was largely sitting idle, and he was anxious to somehow get his Royal Navy more involved in the land fighting.

The Landships Committee was established to develop a fighting vehicle, and it was this artifact that eventually created the name tank. In 1903, H. G. Wells had published *The Land Ironclads* that described large armored vehicles. This created something of a furor in the security services, so a code name had to be adopted. The story was spread that the box-like vehicles were water carriers for use in the Middle East. Unfortunately the abbreviation would be WC (British for a "water closet" or toilet) so "tank" was adopted instead.

Several early prototypes failed until William Tritton developed a drive system based on the American Bullock Creeping Grip Tractor. The prototype was christened Little Willie, a derogatory nickname for the German Crown Prince. A rotating gun turret was considered but quickly abandoned, as it raised the center of gravity with the risk of overturning. After Little Willie proved unsatisfactory, Lieutenant Walter G. Wilson suggested the rhomboid track frame characteristic of British tanks, with the track return passing up and over the top of the vehicle. The prototype was known as "His Majesty's Landship Centipede" and "Big Willie" until the name "Mother" stuck.

After the Army belatedly became involved, naval influence declined, but naval terminology remained permanently attached to tanks: hull, turret, sponson, deck, bow, et cetera. Under the Army's influence it was decided that a variety of armaments would

*Most British tank designs were the characteristic "rhomboid." Designed for crossing trenches and obstacles, the design was far from practical in mobile warfare. The Germans were always lacking in sufficient numbers of tanks, and have pressed this captured British tank into service. (U.S.M.C. History Division)*

be mounted for destroying enemy machine-gun positions. One problem was that the rhomboid design severely limited the fields of fire for weapons mounted in the hull. As a solution, armament was mounted in awkward sponsons that protruded from the sides, a feature then common for the secondary batteries on large warships.

## British Tank Doctrine

For all their pioneering work in developing the first operational tanks, the British Army continued to perceive the tank as the solution to a specific tactical problem—breaching trench lines. Rather than massing tanks, they were typically allocated in small groups with seldom more than 30 vehicles—and often as few as eight—allocated to an army group. The postwar writings of J. F. C. Fuller, who was to become one of the leading advocates of armored warfare, reflect this strictly local tactical mindset.

Even the fundamental design features of British tanks reflected the trench-breaching doctrine, and the rhomboid design of most British tanks limited performance in open warfare.

# The French Heavy Tank Program

The significance of the French tank program has been largely ignored. Jean-Baptiste Estienne was one of the shining lights of the French Army, and turned his fertile mind to the protection of infantry from machine-gun fire. In a staff presentation he predicted that "… the victory in this war will belong to which of the two belligerents which will be the first to place a gun of 75 [mm] on a vehicle able to be driven on all terrain."

What Estienne was not aware of was that the French government was working at cross-purposes. Since May 1915 the Schneider Company was at work on a barbed-wire breaching vehicle. Sergeant Jacques Quellennec had seen men pointlessly slaughtered in the first battle of the Marne, and used his contacts—his father, engineer Edouard Quellennec, mechanic Charles Marius Fouche of the Service Automobile, and Eugene Brillie of the Schneider Company and designer of armored cars, to push forward his ideas for a tracked armored vehicle.

In early December 1915 Estienne and Philippe Pétain witnessed a test of the prototype of the new Schneider CA (later CA 1) tank. It was designed primarily for flattening barbed wire, with a secondary role to eliminate enemy machine-gun positions. Estienne immediately grasped the vehicle's potential, and quickly had a more strategically decisive role in mind.

By mid-December Estienne had proposed formation of an armored force, and drawn up specifications for the vehicle's capabilities, including that of towing an armored sled carrying 20 infantrymen. In late December Estienne met with industrialist Louis Renault, who declined any involvement, saying his firm was overcommitted to producing other vehicles.

Development continued until early 1916, when a dispute led Schneider and the French Army to part ways. Schneider went on to produce the Schneider CA heavy tank, clearly a derivative of the Holt, with a boxy armored body, a boat-like prow for crushing barbed wire, and a short-barreled 75-mm Blockhaus Schneider mounted in a barbette on the right side. The distinctive feature

*The original French heavy tanks were designed primarily for breaching wire obstacles. The prominent horn on the Schneider CA was to push higher wire down and under the tracks. (Association du Souvenir de Sommepy-Tahure)*

of the Schneider was a huge piece of angle iron protruding like a horn from the bow.

There were improvements based on combat experience, and the redesign and conversion of older vehicles continued until the end of the war. The more prominent changes included spaced armor (two plates with an air space between) to defeat German armor-piercing rifle rounds. The internal fuel tanks turned the tank into a death trap when holed by German weapons, so the fuel tanks were moved to the rear and outside the main compartment. As with all tanks of the period the engine was located inside the crew compartment for ready access. A new ventilation system was provided, which meant that crews no longer began to succumb to carbon monoxide poisoning after about an hour of operation. Production of the Schneider was spotty, in part because effort was focussed on producing spare parts for existing vehicles, but largely because production capacity was diverted to artillery tractors.

A competing Army design became the St. Chamond, intended to upstage the Schneider by being larger and heavier. The new tank was designed around a specially designed Canon de 75-mm TR

Saint Chamond mounted to fire through the bow plate, and four machine guns as opposed to the two of the Schneider. A 90 hp petrol engine generated power for two electric motors. The design made for much easier steering and more torque at low speeds, but could not remedy the fact that the vehicle was underpowered, and that the elongated bow limited trench-crossing capability.

When the new tank was tested in April 1916, major problems were the tank's ergonomics. The driver sat high above the ground with his head and shoulders in a cupola on the left front roof. A second cupola blocked vision to the right, but worst of all, the isolated driver also functioned as tank commander, a ridiculous combination of responsibilities.

Estienne knew nothing about the competing designs. His elation at an order for 400 new heavy tanks turned to dismay when he learned the design details: "I am painfully surprised that an order of this importance has been placed without asking the opinion of the only officer who, at the time had undertaken a detailed study of the technical and military aspects involved…."

*The St. Chamond heavy tank had a bow-mounted 75-mm field gun. The design, with two cupolas, severely limited the driver/tank commander's vision to the right. (Association du Souvenir de Sommepy-Tahure)*

Early use of the tank in combat revealed additional problems, and there were continuous modifications to the St. Chamond, particularly conversion to the standard French 75-mm field gun. A sloping roof was designed to counter the German tactic of throwing satchel charges onto the top, and elimination of the second cupola. But nothing could remedy the tank's fundamental design flaws. In the final stages of the war the St. Chamond found its niche as an assault gun.

Although some of his design concepts were incorporated, Estienne played no role in the final technical development. He had instead turned his efforts to resolving the thousands of details necessary to bring the tank to maturity, from refining doctrine, to establishing training facilities, and assuring a flow of spare parts. His championship of the new idea and organizational skills earned him the title of the father of the French armored forces.

## The French Light Tank Program

The tank idea planted in Louis Renault's mind had continued to stir. Estienne and Renault met again on July 16, 1916 and Renault himself later drew up the basic specifications of a vehicle that would influence tank design for the next century. Then he unleashed his most talented design and production experts. The result was the revolutionary FT, for *faible tonnage*, or light tonnage. (The vehicle is often erroneously called the FT-17, a term that somehow became commonplace in the 1940s, but was never an official name.)

A doctrinal question soon arose as to whether a few heavy tanks were more effective than a swarm of the new Renault tanks, so Estienne at first expressed opposition to the new design. But on November 27, 1916, Estienne sent a memorandum recommending adoption of the Renault design.

Demand for the light tank to equip French, and later American, formations was so great that the vehicle was eventually produced by four manufacturers, including competitor Schneider. An

American redesign, the M1918, included conversion to English measurements for details like bolts and screws, replacement of the large wooden front idler wheel with a steel one, and a more reliable Buda diesel engine. The latter feature allowed the addition of a much-appreciated firewall.

The FT was eventually exported to several countries, and in turn some were passed along to secondary users. Users eventually included Afghanistan, Belgium, Brazil, China, Czechoslovakia, Estonia, Finland, Nazi Germany, Iran, Japan, Lithuania, the Netherlands, the Philippines, Poland, Romania, White Russian forces and later the Soviet Union, Spain, Sweden, Switzerland, Turkey, the United Kingdom, and Yugoslavia. The M1918 was used by the United States Army and Marine Corps in the 1920s and 1930s, and by Canada as a training vehicle in World War II. Derivatives included the Italian Fiat 3000, Soviet "Russki Reno" (a blatant, unlicensed copy), and the Soviet T-18 with a redesigned suspension.

# Communications and Evolving Doctrine

A serious problem was the lack of communications between vehicles. Crews were briefed on the mission, and thereafter might play follow the leader if the plan had to be adjusted on the fly. The only practical means of communication with other tanks was by colored signal flags or colored discs poked out a small signal hatch, semaphore masts mounted on the top of unit leaders' tanks, or colored lamps. One-way communications to the rear were provided by human runners or homing pigeons, but most pigeons asphyxiated: for humans "the stay in the tanks mustn't exceed 24 hours" stated a 1918 French report.

The various armies experimented with radios, but sets were bulky, easily damaged, and had only a short range. Two Schneider tanks were converted by addition of radios and 13-meter antenna masts. The Renault FT was too small to accommodate a radio, so a special

The specifications for the new **Renault tank** were that the vehicle would weigh no more than 7 tons so it could be transported by truck. A new engine was designed, and tracks would be automatically kept under the proper tension to avoid the thrown tracks that plagued so many tanks. The engine would draw cooling air through the crew space and exhaust it to the rear.

The greatest innovation of all was the general layout: the driver sat low and to the front with an excellent field of vision, the engine was to the rear, and a rotating turret gave the single turret-mounted weapon a 360-degree field of fire. It would have only a single weapon, a Hotchkiss heavy machine gun, and in later versions a Puteaux 37-mm cannon. The only problems were that the crew comprised only two men, which meant that the vehicle commander/gunner/loader was overburdened, there was no firewall separating the crew space from the hot engine, and the engine was initially plagued by fan-belt problems. However the design proved so robust that it remained essentially unchanged except for a new welded turret that was simpler to produce than the original cast version.

variant, the TSF (*Transmission sans fil*) was introduced that replaced the turret with a large, boxy superstructure for the radio gear.

The development of communications vehicles was being driven by an evolving doctrine. The arrival of the fast light British "cruiser tanks" like the Whippet and the French FT forced a major reconsideration of doctrine. Once the enemy front lines were breached, what was the role of the tank? Could the unique mobility of the tank make it a replacement for the cavalry? Estienne, like

*The first practical communications vehicle, the FT Transmission Sans Fils radio tank was unarmed, characterized by a fixed superstructure and a three-man crew. This American M1918 variant is identifiable by the large slid-steel front idler wheel. (U.S.M.C. History Division)*

other tank visionaries, foresaw an overwhelming swarm of light tanks spearheading the exploitation phase of battle. If so, rapid and reliable communications would be required.

# The German Effort

The German high command remained skeptical of the tank, even after encounters with British tanks. As a result, German tank design and production was too little and too late.

German designers seized upon the Holt artillery tractor as the chassis, and the rest of the design harkened back to Kaiser Wilhelm's mobile fortress. The tall, lumbering A7V with its tiny tracks originally bristled with two cannons and four machine guns. The high profile would plague the vehicle; it was prone to overturning and indeed most losses resulted from such mishaps.

A re-design eliminated the rear-firing cannon, and the final armament was a single front-mounted 57-mm cannon and six machine guns. The 17–18-man crew was directed by an officer who sat, with the driver, in a roof cupola high above the ground with very poor vision to the front.

German design and production lagged behind the Allies, and Daimler did not deliver the first operational A7V Sturmpanzerwagen until October 1917. Germany produced a paltry 64 of these vehicles, and one was an unarmored Überlandwagen supply carrier. The A7V was always committed in limited numbers, with only five in its first action on March 21, 1918. That day only two actually saw action; the other three suffered mechanical breakdowns.

German efforts to develop larger and more modern designs never got beyond the prototype stage. Development of German tanks and a coherent doctrine for their use would eventually come from the lower ranks.

## Imperial Russia

Designers in Russia quickly jumped on the armored vehicle design bandwagon, producing several design concepts but only two known prototypes.

The first attempt, not truly a tank in the usual sense, is worthy of a closer look simply because it was so bizarre. The 1914 Tsar Tank used an innovative but flawed electrically driven reverse-tricycle concept. Two gigantic spoked wheels some 9 meters in diameter were powered by electrical motors through chain drives. A smaller 1.5-meter trailing roller supported the rear. The entire layout was quite similar to a 19th-century artillery carriage, and was designed to simply roll over obstacles. An armored cannon turret sat on a tower atop the carriage aft of the main wheels. Additional cannon were located in sponsons that protruded from the sides, and machine-gun positions beneath the superstructure provided for protection against infantry.

The fundamental flaw should have been apparent: the frail wheels and chain drive were too vulnerable to enemy fire. Although electric motors are well suited to produce the high torque necessary to pull a vehicle over obstacles, the Tsar Tank's motors were not powerful enough to pull free the heavy trailing wheel, which had a tendency to sink into the ground. Field tests in August 1915 were a fiasco, and the vehicle was abandoned in place.

The automobile-sized 1915 Vezdekhod ("goes anywhere") is often depicted in tank histories, but extant drawings and a photograph suggest it was intended as a small all-terrain transport.

## The Tanks go to War

The British were the first nation to use tanks in combat, and the first to squander their potential. On July 1, 1916, Sir Douglas Haig launched 100,000 British troops in a massive assault, the battle of the Somme, to support French offensives and drive back the Germans. By day's end 60,000 infantry were dead, wounded, or missing and presumed dead. Unwilling to accept failure, Haig continued to batter at the Germans for weeks.

As the offensive faltered, the British decided to test the potential of the new tanks. There were 49 Mark I tanks available, but only 36 in working order. On September 15, the tanks made their combat debut. Instead of a mass attack they were scattered in support of several divisions.

The battle of Flers-Courcelette was a typical small component, as tanks fought in small groups attached to infantry brigades. A powerful artillery bombardment was plotted to keep open "tank lanes" so that the vehicles could advance with less chance of falling into craters. The misadventures of ten tanks operating with the British First Guards Brigade were typical. One failed to start, others suffered mechanical failures, some wandered off into the adjacent division's zone, others ran into ditches, and the sole survivor ran short of fuel. The tank lane concept failed when tanks lost their way.

Tanks operating with the British 47th Division were ordered to support an attack on a position called High Wood. The corps commander ignored repeated objections that the tanks would have to advance through terrain littered with broken stumps and fallen trees—only one survived the obstacles.

Many of the German infantry panicked and surrendered at the sight of the mechanical monsters, but others stood firm. Machine guns and artillery deluged the tanks with fire. Tank D1 earned the distinction of being the first tank put out of action by enemy fire when it was hit by an artillery shell. The Germans had already developed armor-piercing rounds for rifles and machine guns, designed to counter the small steel shields used by artillery observers and snipers. These were turned upon the tanks.

The tank crews quickly discovered that even if enemy fire did not penetrate the armor, it sent spall—splinters of the tank's own paint or even steel armor—flying about the interior. Machine-gun and rifle fire that did not even dent the armor created "splash," droplets of molten lead generated when a bullet's kinetic energy was instantly converted into thermal energy. Splash entered through vision slits, joints and rivet holes, or any other tiny opening in the armor.

One British tank officer described to new American arrivals what it was like to be under intense fire. Even the smallest of spall flakes stung and penetrated exposed skin. Then "simultaneously with the sound of impact and creation of the flakes, a blue flame is seen, and when a machine-gun plays up and down the joints" the interior "looks like demonstration of cheap fireworks."

Isolated tanks were set upon by German hand bombers (grenadiers), one immobilized tank held the enemy infantry at bay for five hours before being set afire. Infantry coordination was poor, and in at least one case the tanks fired on their own infantry until an officer ran up to the tank and redirected its attack.

In cases where the tanks reached the enemy lines, they proved useful in eliminating machine-gun positions. Overall the effort failed, primarily from the tanks becoming stuck in ditches, through mechanical failures, and the inability of the infantry to move forward in support.

# Tanks in Penny-Packets

High-ranking British officers persisted in using the tanks piecemeal as described in a 1928 Master's degree thesis by American Captain Dale Wilson:

> On 16 November the British used two tanks to lead the attack at Beaumont-Hamel. One crossed the Germans' frontline trench and became stuck, while the other became mired in front of the trench. Despite this fiasco, the Germans were so shocked by the tanks' appearance on the battlefield that soldiers in both the frontline and supporting trenches began waving white cloths to signal their surrender. The tank crews and supporting infantry were able to capture the entire garrison before the Germans could discover that the tanks were immobilized and all but at their mercy.

Eventually senior officers accepted the idea of using tanks in mass, and on November 20, 1917, a force of 350 (some sources cite over 400) participated in the battle of Cambrai. Cambrai is often cited as the first decisive action for tanks, but the true contribution of the tanks is difficult to assess. German troops had by then been specially trained in antitank tactics, and were veterans of fighting against French tanks in the Nivelle Offensive in April–May 1917.

The first day's combat was a stunning success, due more to the element of surprise than any other. The British failed to achieve their objectives, but some units penetrated as much as 8 kilometers. The victory had taken a heavy toll. Sixty-five tanks had been destroyed by enemy action, 71 were lost to mechanical failures, and 43 had ditched. The Germans quickly rushed reinforcements to stem the rout, and the British paused to consolidate their gains.

On November 23, a renewed attack supported by about 100 surviving tanks failed to achieve even local objectives. On November 27, one final effort, supported by about 30 tanks, achieved the final objective—the crest of Bourlon Ridge—but was driven off by a counterattack.

The offensive had been a spectacular success by Western Front standards, and helped stifle criticism of the tanks as ineffective. The Germans also acknowledged the potential of the tanks: "Wherever the ground is suitable for tanks, surprise attacks like this may be expected" (Crown Prince Rupprecht, Commander, Army Group Rupprecht). The following year would indeed see massive tank attacks, made possible by the Renault light tank. It would become part of all major Allied offensives, starting on May 31, 1918 with the commitment of about thirty FTs in the battle of Chaudun.

## The First Tank-on-Tank Battle

There was little perceived chance of encountering the enemy's tanks, so there was no reason to equip tanks with any of the armor-piercing ammunition used by the artillery or infantry.

The second battle of Villers-Bretonneux was a sub-action of the battle of Lys, April 24–26, 1918, part of the great German offensive of 1918. After two days of shelling, the Germans launched an attack on the village with four divisions but only 13 tanks. The capture of the village threatened a crucial railway junction at Amiens, so three British tanks from the Number 1 Section, A Company, 1st Battalion, Tank Corps were dispatched to support a counterattack. The section was led by Lieutenant Frank Mitchell in a Mark IV Male, with two Mark IV Females. Several of the new British Whippet light tanks, designed to fill the role of cavalry if a breakthrough could be achieved, were in reserve.

The British tanks encountered A7V *Nixe* (Number 561) of Abteilung III commanded by Lieutenant Wilhelm Biltz. Two other A7Vs were nearby, but Biltz had already lost Number 506 *Mephisto* in a shell hole. The two Females engaged *Nixe*. Their machine guns were ineffective, but return fire from *Nixe*'s cannon ruptured the armor of both British tanks. Mitchell kept his Male on the move, trying to evade fire from German field guns—much more dangerous than *Nixe*'s small cannon. Mitchell stopped to allow his gunner a clear shot and his gunner quickly scored several hits. As

Biltz maneuvered to avoid the fire *Nixe* slid sideways into a ditch.

The German crew abandoned the tank. Two more A7Vs supported by infantry arrived, but when Mitchell opened fire the German tanks fled, abandoning their infantry. Mitchell turned his attention to the enemy infantry, firing canister, a shell containing numerous steel balls. As Mitchell was working considerable slaughter, seven Whippets arrived and charged into the German infantry. The Whippets ruthlessly machine-gunned the infantry, crushing many under their tracks. German field guns destroyed three of the smaller tanks, and when the rest withdrew, Mitchell observed that their tracks were covered with blood.

The German field guns turned their full fury on Mitchell's tank. A shell broke a track, and the crew bailed out and took refuge in a nearby British trench. Some months later British and Australian troops recovered *Mephisto*. It is currently on display in Canberra, the only surviving A7V.

## Late Arrivals: The Americans

By early 1917 Allied tank doctrine had crystallized into two camps. In a contentious May 1917 meeting in London the British argued for distributing heavy tanks among infantry formations. The French concept was to hold the versatile FTs as a massed tactical reserve to be called forward if an infantry assault bogged down. Although the French doctrine was more sophisticated, both perceived the tank as a solution to a localized tactical problem.

The United States came late to the Great War in April 1917, but its massive industrial potential boded well for Allied fortunes. The American love affair with mechanization made the tank a natural focus of interest, but early reports had branded the tank as a failure. Nonetheless, in early 1917 the chief of the U.S. Army War College directed the head of the American mission in France to report on British and French tank doctrine. The May 21 report included the personal observations of Major Frank H. Parker, and profoundly affected the future of tanks in the U.S. Army.

Some of General John J. Pershing's more unimaginative officers recommended a mixed force of British heavy and French light tanks for the American Expeditionary Force (AEF). On September 1, a tank board appointed by Pershing made its recommendation: a separate tank force with a director reporting directly to Pershing. The Tank Corps was to be a mixed force of 30 companies with 2,000 Renault FT and 15 companies with 200 British Mark VI heavy tanks, the latter still in the design stage. The tanks were to be organized into 21 light tank battalions (77 tanks each) and eight heavy tank battalions (45 tanks each).

The tank board's recommendations reflected determination to restore mobility to the battlefield, and the report paid close attention to the nuts and bolts of logistics, communications, and creation of an all-arms force. Most offensives had foundered on the logistical and communications difficulties encountered once a tactical breakthrough had been achieved.

Every breakthrough on the Western Front had failed because artillery left the ground churned and cratered, with roads obliterated and telephone line networks shredded. Supplies to maintain tactical momentum could not be moved through this lunar landscape. Commanders usually had no idea where their advancing units were, with no way to coordinate the continuation of an offensive. The movement of horse-drawn artillery was simply impossible. As a consequence the British in particular continued to rely upon a tactical model wherein the tanks retreated to fixed supply points when fuel and ammunition were depleted.

The American recommendations were a decade ahead of their allies. The final report called for:

> 350 heavy tanks of British Mark VI pattern; 20 similar tanks equipped for [radio] signal purposes; 40 similar tanks for supply of gasoline and oil; 140 tanks arranged to carry 25 soldiers or five tons of supplies; 50 similar tanks with upper platform for field gun; total 600 heavy tanks. Also following Renault tanks: 1,030 for fighting purposes; 130 for supply; 40 for [radio] signal purposes; total 1,200 Renault tanks.

The report recommended that the Mark VI be acquired in Male and Female versions. Of the Renaults, two-thirds would be equipped with machine guns, the others with 6-pounder (57-mm) or 3-inch (75-mm) cannon. (Exactly how the big cannons were to be mounted in the tiny Renaults was not explained.) Renault tanks (as the M1918) and the Mark VI were to be produced in America. The overall coordinator of Allied tank production cancelled the Mark VI in favor of the Mark VIII, but in truth the Americans were not happy with the poor mechanical reliability of any of the heavy tanks—British or French.

The new tank corps caught the attention of a young disgruntled cavalry captain on Pershing's staff, George S. Patton. Patton met Colonel Fox Conner (best known as Dwight Eisenhower's mentor) who encouraged Patton to consider tanks as opposed to an infantry battalion command. Patton solicited Pershing's approval, noting that the proposed use of light tanks would be "analogous to the duty performed by cavalry," his experience as a machine-gun unit commander, his command of the French language, and above all his experience as "the only American who has ever made an attack in a motor vehicle." This last referred to a minor fracas in Mexico on May 14, 1916 when Patton and ten soldiers from the 6th Infantry, with two civilian guides, were on patrol in three 1915 Dodge touring cars.

On November 10, 1917, Patton was assigned to establish an American light tank school. His only assistant was First Lieutenant Elgin Braine, who was destined to play a large but unremembered role in the development of the American tank program. Patton threw himself into the task. In August 1918 he assumed command of the First Provisional Tank Brigade (later renamed 304th Tank Brigade). He became the first American to drive a tank and learn the operation of its various components. Patton's enthusiasm was due more to personal ambition than to military zeal. In a letter to his wife he wrote candidly that "no one knows anything about the subject except me. I am certainly in on the ground floor. If they are a success I may have the chance I have always been looking for."

Patton's final report was groundbreaking in that it covered not only the technical aspects of tanks, but training, organization, support functions, tactics, and doctrine. He recommend "first echelon" repair capabilities at the company level. The practice of establishing what maintenance and repairs would be done at what level would become a defining factor in American tank doctrine. He recommended organic transport at battalion level, with heavy trucks and trailers capable of moving the light tanks: the shortage of heavy trucks had often hampered the Allies' assembly of tank forces. Each tank company would have a separate command vehicle to allow the commander to accompany his unit into battle as opposed to relying entirely upon a fixed plan, a radio tank, and eight tanks fitted as supply and ammunition carriers.

One of his tactical recommendations, the five-tank platoon with three platoons to a company, remained the basis for American unit organization for nearly a century. The organization simplified coordination with infantry; one platoon to support each infantry company, a company to support each battalion. He recommended personal reconnaissance by unit officers, and that whenever possible unit commanders be given the opportunity to view the terrain from aircraft. This last recommendation would not be routinely implemented until 1944, in the Pacific.

The list of technical improvements was exhaustive, including such overlooked details as a lock for the engine compartment (to keep the enemy from prying it open), non-skid floor mats, and tow chains. One was a feature for which tank crewmen would be eternally grateful—an improved hard leather helmet to protect their heads.

Patton recognized that the primary task for the tank was breaching the enemy's defenses, but that the role should then transition seamlessly into the traditional role of the cavalry to "ride the enemy to death."

The organization of the heavy tank units was irrevocably tied to the British program, so training was conducted at Bovington Camp in Dorset. A call for tank volunteers was answered by a strange assortment, including "two gold miners, three Boer War veterans, three pugilists, six members of last year's football team at Williams College, six former United States Marines, three men who had won the French Croix de Guerre, a filibuster ["a person engaging in unauthorized warfare against a foreign country"], an Argentine cavalryman, a dancing master, a lion tamer, and forty men from the University of Chicago …"

One of the men organizing the heavy tank battalions was Captain Dwight D. Eisenhower. But when the first battalion was shipped to England "My chief said he was impressed by my 'organizational ability'. I was directed to take the remnants of the troops who would not be going overseas, and proceed to an old, abandoned campsite in Gettysburg, Pennsylvania, of all places." These "remnants" would be the cadre for the 302nd Tank Battalion.

The training at Bovington was comprehensive, but the highlight was driver training. To steer the British Mark IV required two drivers, one to operate the gears for each track. One crewman wrote of:

> … the thrill of pulling a monster out of a deep trench, the nose pointing at the sky with the engine's deafening roar, the acrid, never-to-be-forgotten smell of exploded [exhaust] gas, scorching oil and grease, and hot steel, the quick shutting down of the throttle, the gentle swing to earth, and then the triumphant roaring answer of the engine to the opening of the throttle and the more-the-merry clanking of the track plates.

The Americans did not endear themselves to their experienced British instructors, primarily by questioning the British doctrine for longer-term operations once German defenses had been breached.

Patton's lack of tanks to occupy the growing force of idle men was almost his undoing. He then hit upon the idea of practicing maneuvers without tanks. The men were divided into crews, who walked through exercises in "machine foot drills," practicing signals, directions from tank commander/gunner to driver, and other operational necessities. The first ten FTs arrived on March 23, 1918. In late May and early June Patton and other officers toured a section of the front, talking with men from the American 1st Division and the French tanks that had supported them at Cantigny, on May 28–31.

Patton was dismayed by rumors that another newly arrived senior officer would be given command of the new tank force. Colonel Samuel D. Rockenbach, Pershing's staff officer in charge of the tank program, and no friend of Patton, gave the new officer a frigid reception, and recommended Patton. On August 20, 1918, Patton was ordered to assume command of the new tank brigade.

Patton's brigade first saw action in the effort to reduce the St. Mihiel salient and recapture the city of Metz, September 12–15, 1918. In addition to the American brigade, French light and heavy tanks supported the attack. The offensive followed the French tactical plan, with tanks held in reserve until needed, but stubborn resistance by German rear guards covered a retreat and forced commitment of tanks on the first day. Patton could not control his aggressive instincts and frustration at the slow pace imposed by muddy conditions. He led from the front, sometimes on foot, sometimes riding the front of a tank like a horse in an often vain attempt to catch up with the retreating enemy.

Shortages of American Liberty engines caused delays in the acquisition of heavy tanks, and the British agreed to provide the needed tanks only if the Americans supported British operations. Thus Mark V heavy tanks equipped the 301st Battalion, assigned to the British Fourth Tank Brigade in support of the Australian Corps. Their initial attack on September 29 floundered in typical fashion: liaison with the infantry was poor, some tanks bumbled into an unmapped British minefield, and others were struck by German artillery. In the end only ten tanks survived to support the attack. In all it was not an auspicious beginning for American heavy tanks, and an experience that would be reflected in American tank doctrine for decades.

On September 26, the AEF at last launched an independent offensive into the Argonne Forest, supported by light tanks.

Overall the terrain did not favor tanks, and they played little part in the subsequent fighting.

The rapid collapse of the German Army ended the war, and the extensive planning for an all-arms American tank corps was rendered irrelevant by rapid demobilization.

# The American Design Experience

The Americans were never happy with any of the heavy tank designs they had used during the war, and particularly with the French heavies, which were really mobile artillery. In late 1917 Majors James A. Drain and Herbert W. Alden worked up a joint design with the British, with armor, structural components, and weaponry to be provided by the British, powerful and reliable Liberty aircraft engines and most other related components by the Americans, all to be assembled in French facilities. The new tank, the Mark VIII Liberty, would have a higher horsepower to weight ratio, greater speed, better armor, and seven machine guns and two 6-pounder cannon. The French exhibited no interest in the project, and since the Liberty engines were in high demand for aircraft production the new tanks would not be available until early 1919.

Production of the FT in America proved frustrating. The French agreed to provide plans and two example vehicles, but actually provided only plans and a turret. Lieutenant Elgin Braine, now Patton's right-hand man, was to return to America and oversee the tank manufacturing program. In hindsight, Pershing should have assigned an officer with sufficient rank to battle the Army's bureaucracy. After much effort Braine managed to obtain low-priority passage for himself and the turret aboard an old tramp freighter.

The Army assumed that companies would bid for contracts to build the new tank. Instead, they were inundated with competing designs. One designer, Henry Ford, was never happy with other people's designs, and submitted his own designs for three-man and two-man tanks. The War Department eventually contracted the Maxwell Motor Company and other small companies to build the 1918. Ford pressed on relentlessly, and in early 1918 demonstrated his own tank to the Ordnance Department. Braine was unimpressed, but later learned that the Ordnance Department had notified Pershing that the test was a smashing success.

Braine's efforts continued to be thwarted. The Ordnance Department Engineering Office in Dayton, Ohio and the Ordnance Department Headquarters in Washington worked on competing designs for the turret. Braine was reassigned, instructed to work on design of the new tank in his spare time, and was forbidden to communicate with the contingents in France or with the newly appointed director of the Tank Corps in Washington. Designs were rejected because they were not drafted on the correct paper.

Braine wanted instruments calibrated in the metric system but the Ordnance Department wanted English units. The final compromise was a gauge that measured speed in miles per hour and an odometer that measured travel distance in kilometers. The Ordnance Department decided not to produce the French cannons and machine guns, and new designs necessitated a redesign of the turret. When Braine located unused aircraft machine guns, the Ordnance Department squabbled over details like the pistol grip modification. Exasperated beyond bearing, Braine finally bypassed channels and went directly to the Assistant Secretary of War. But it was the summer of 1918, and too late.

The Ford prototype was shipped to France amid much fanfare, but Pershing was also unimpressed, recommending its use as an artillery tractor. He recommended that the M1918 "be pushed and that no interference with its production be permitted." The first two M1918s arrived in France on November 20, 1918.

In the end, the American tank development program remained limited to the M1918, and further development of more advanced types was stymied by public resistance to a standing army and the Great Depression. The combined-arms force conceived by the Americans would be famously resurrected as the Nazi *panzer* divisions.

# CHAPTER 2

# THE INTER–WAR YEARS

*Adherence to dogmas has destroyed more armies and cost more battles than anything in war.*

Major General J. F. C. Fuller

THE "INTERWAR YEARS" WERE AN ERA of proxy wars among the rising Fascist nations, the Western democracies, and the ascendant Soviets. The French FT was ideally suited to use by less technically advanced users and saw extensive combat in the Russian Civil War, Estonian War of Independence, the Polish–Soviet War, the Rif War, Chinese Civil War, and the Spanish Civil War.

It was a period of general stagnation for military development. The British and French were happy with the doctrines that had won the Great War, and the British saw the Royal Navy and the new Royal Air Force as priorities. Germany was forbidden to own heavy weapons. The Russians were involved in a savage civil war. The Japanese were struggling into the industrial age, hindered by lack of natural resources. The newly powerful Americans withdrew into isolationism. Throwing a pall over the entire world was the Great Depression.

The world was simply not ready for mechanized warfare. Motor vehicles lacked reliability, and motor fuel was often unavailable. In North America and Russia interconnected road networks were virtually non-existent outside of cities.

# France

The losers of a war learn most from analysis of the causes of their defeat, while the winners often slide into complacency. The French Army emerged from the Great War as the leading practitioner of armored warfare, with above all a tested tank doctrine. Unfortunately the French prepared to fight the next war with fixed defenses and massed infantry. Strategic doctrine advocated by Philippe Pétain decreed that tanks would be parceled out in small groups controlled by the infantry.

The main dissenting voice was the obnoxious Colonel Charles De Gaulle. His book, *Vers l'Armée de Métier* (*Toward a Professional Army*) advocated the use of tanks and mechanized infantry. The book was a failure in France, but a German translation sold ten times as many copies.

France continued to develop tank designs that were quite modern in concept. French industry pioneered production of cast hulls and turrets, which speeded production. The Hotchkiss H35 armed with a 37-mm cannon and 7.62-mm machine gun was later upgraded to the H39. French doctrine did not consider it a problem, but the design retained the overworked tank commander/gunner in his one-man turret. The more advanced Somua S35 cavalry tank was armed with a 47-mm cannon and a machine gun, and had a three-man crew. The S35 outclassed its foremost future foes. It could reliably destroy the Panzer I at ranges up to a kilometer, and was relatively immune to the cannon of the Panzer III at normal combat ranges. Problems of both designs were high cost, poor mechanical reliability, difficulty of repair, and the absence of radios and intercoms.

The Chars de Bataille B1 and B1 bis heavy infantry tanks were conceived as "breakthrough" assault vehicles. Primary armament was a 75-mm howitzer firing only forward. A small machine-gun turret provided defense against enemy infantry, and later a 47-mm cannon in a larger turret allowed engagement of enemy armor. The B1 was impervious to almost all German guns, but slow speed and appetite for fuel rendered it impractical for a war of swift movement.

French efforts were hampered by continuing doctrinal battles. The infantry had tanks (*chars*) but the cavalry had *automitrailleuses* (self-propelled machine guns)—often the same vehicles. There was infighting between advocates of the heavy infantry tank, and officers like de Gaulle who wanted swarms of light tanks. France knew that war with Germany was imminent, and began preparation for a war anticipated to begin in 1941. But Germany struck first.

# Britain

The British tank corps had fallen into the doldrums. The chief advocate was Colonel J. F. C. Fuller, who in the closing days of the war formulated Plan 1919 that combined aircraft and mechanized forces with German *sturmtaktiks*. Still, British doctrine remained tactical in scope, as indicated by Fuller's 1920 *Tanks in the Great War*.

The British created an experimental mechanized force in May 1927; Fuller was refused the command in favor of infantry Colonel R. J. Collins. The unit tested hardware like the Vickers Medium Mark I tank with a turret-mounted 47-mm gun, the innovative 84-mm Birch Gun (the first practical self-propelled artillery piece), and tactical control by radio. The force was dissolved in 1928, and a "Mobile Division" not created until November 1937. Once commenced, mechanization was rapid and most cavalry regiments were mechanized by 1939. Higher leadership was still reluctant to accept the tank as a potentially decisive system, and the British Expeditionary Force sent to France in 1939 included only two tank battalions to support nine infantry divisions.

# The Soviet Union

The Soviet Union was being dragged into the modern age by a series of five-year plans. Tank production was a boon to the burgeoning vehicle industry, since there was no civilian market.

The Soviets borrowed heavily from Western technology and production methods. One of the most significant was the acquisition of a T3 experimental tank chassis designed by the American J. Walter Christie, with an innovative suspension that allowed a tank to move across rough terrain at high speeds. The resulting BT Fast Tanks (BT-2, BT-5, BT-7 and BT-7M) were reliable, armed with a good 45-mm main gun, and as many as 8,600 may have been built. Soon the Soviet Union had more tanks than the rest of the world combined, with a tank battalion organic to each infantry division. In 1934 two mechanized corps were stood up, with 430 tanks each.

Soviet doctrine was driven by Marshal Mikhail Tukhachevsky, an early champion of Vladimir Triandafillov's *glubokaya operatsiya* ("deep battle theory"). The doctrine also owed much to Georgii Samoilovich Isserson, much of whose work remains classified by the Russian government. The doctrine envisioned large-scale rupture of the enemy defense, 70–80 km in width, followed by equally deep penetrations by all-arms forces. Triandafillov: "The effect of this mental state leads to operational shock or system paralysis…" Paralysis rather than attrition flew in the face of previous Russian doctrine based on extravagant expenditure of manpower. The theory was also sophisticated in that it saw deep battle as not just a tactical theory, but encompassing geopolitical objectives. Deep battle theory became official Soviet doctrine in 1936. The implementation was halted by the 1936–38 Stalinist purges: Tukhachevsky was shot on June 12, 1937.

# America

The lessons from the American 1918 tank production fiasco proved pivotal in the next war. In 1928 the Assistant Director of the Army Industrial College read Lieutenant Braine's 1918 report. He concluded that the tank procurement program was

> … a fine example of lack of industrial planning and a horrible commentary on our preparedness when we entered the last war. The records of our branches are full of this sort of data—unfortunately not as forcibly stated in many cases. It is on data of this sort that we are getting the details of things we must plan to avoid in our next war …

In addition to Patton and Eisenhower, Sereno E. Brett played a pivotal role in development of mechanized doctrine. Despite his contributions, Brett never attained high rank. The 1919 Transcontinental Motor Convoy played a little known but crucial role in development of American armored doctrine. Under Eisenhower and Brett's command, the convoy traveled from Washington DC to San Francisco over 5,230 km (3,250 miles) of largely unpaved and unmapped roads. Important lessons were that vehicles had to be simple to operate, robust, and mechanically reliable. This experience led the U.S. Army to a mechanized doctrine that emphasized mechanical reliability, simplicity of operation and repair, and sheer numbers to replace attrition.

American development of both tanks and doctrine was hampered by the successes of World War I. Large stocks of M1918s hindered development of new designs well into the 1930s, since there was no perceived need for new tanks. The U.S. Army was very rigidly divided into separate branches, and tanks were seen solely as adjuncts, direct support weapons for infantry. A 1920 directive from the Command and General Staff College:

> The tank should be recognized as an infantry supporting and accompanying weapon, incapable of independent, decisive, strategic, and generally, tactical action. The infantry, or other formed troops, must accompany or immediately follow tanks. Otherwise no ground will be held … There is no such thing as an independent tank attack.

It went on to state that the tank's sole role was to "… facilitate the uninterrupted advance of the rifleman …." As late as 1938 an

*This M3 light tank undergoing maintenance was typical of American light tanks of the 1930s. (U.S.M.C. via Ken Estes)*

infantry doctrinal manual made it clear that the tank had a very circumscribed support role, and the Infantry Branch remained locked into a trench warfare mentality. The cavalry was the force for fast-moving exploitation, but although senior officers foresaw the potential for future wars of maneuver, there was a total doctrinal disjoint. Like the French, in a legal nicety identical tracked fighting vehicles belonging to the cavalry became "combat cars."

By the mid-1930s the motor vehicle was rendering the horse obsolete. The first experimental mechanized cavalry regiment was well ahead of its time in including mobile infantry, artillery, engineers, and aviation assets, but the idea met resistance from the horsey set as neatly explained by Colonel Adna Chaffee Jr.:

> They seem blind to the possibilities of a mechanized cavalry.... The definition of cavalry includes troops of any kind equipped for highly mobile combat and not just mounted on horses. The motto of the [Cavalry] School is "Through Mobility We Conquer." It does not say, "Through Mobility On Horses Alone We Conquer."

By 1937 there were only two mechanized cavalry regiments, and thirteen horse regiments. There were also more sordid reasons for the resistance. By 1940 heads of both the Infantry and Cavalry Branches still saw the creation of an armored force as a threat to their funding. As justification, both seized upon the successes of antitank guns in the Spanish Civil War as evidence that the tank had no future.

# Germany

Germany learned much from its crushing 1918 defeat, but the militarists refused to acknowledge the reasons for that defeat. They seized upon the "stab in the back" theory: Germany had not been brought down by military defeat, but by internal subversion. Skirting the provisions of the Treaty of Versailles, in 1926 the military began to develop clandestine rearmament plans, directed by Commander-in-Chief Hans von Seeckt. They were aided by the new Soviet Union, which made available testing facilities at Kama. German industrial firms were encouraged in the production of prototypes under code names.

Germany still faced the basic problem that brought it down in 1918. It simply did not have the manpower, natural resources, or industrial capacity to compete with America and the Soviet Union. A German remedy would be to substitute advanced technology and qualitative superiority for numbers. Unfortunately German production practices were based on teams of craftsmen who constructed a tank or aircraft, often crafting or modifying individual parts. Unlike the Soviets, the Germans were slow to adopt the American concept of the production line.

A new German tank doctrine was pioneered by General Oswald Lutz and his chief-of-staff Lieutenant Colonel Heinz Guderian. Although it is not clear how much Guderian was influenced by inter-war theoreticians, his concepts for a combined-arms force followed the typical plan. The *panzerkorps* would include heavy tanks to support an infantry breakthrough, and light tanks for exploitation. The place where German doctrine parted ways was

*The Panzer I, the size of a small automobile and armed with two machine guns, was the backbone of the panzer divisions in Poland and France. (Gilbert)*

in the call for a super-heavy tank. The French Maginot Line was much on the mind of German planners, and the plan proposed a 100-ton tank with a 150-mm main gun. It was beyond the technical and manufacturing capabilities of any nation, but exposed a growing German fascination with gigantism.

Hamstrung by economics and industrial limitations, Germany briefly took a step backward from its own doctrine, placing emphasis upon numbers of less expensive light tanks. The small Panzer IA tank, with two machine guns, was Germany's first mass-produced tank. Entering service in 1934, it was intended to train crews and test manufacturing capabilities, but it was Germany's primary tank when Hitler repudiated the Versailles treaty. The Panzer I was outclassed by the old FT, but would serve to develop and test doctrine.

In its quest for qualitative superiority, Germany developed new tank types, introducing the Panzer II (one 20-mm cannon, one machine gun) in 1938. The 1939 Panzer III was the first design intended to fight other tanks. Designed to accommodate a 50-mm gun, the initial models instead carried the infantry's 37-mm antitank weapon. The first medium tank was the Panzer

> An important doctrinal innovation of the German Army was the **kampfgruppe** (battle group), a brigade-sized unit that could be task-organized from available units. The *kampfgruppen* would be combined-arms teams based loosely on German organizational practices developed in the Geat War, and the 1918 American model, but without the fixed structure.

IV, with a short-barreled low-velocity 75-mm gun intended for infantry support.

Limited industrial capacity and the Great Depression hampered development of a true mechanized force. The new SdKfz151 (1939) and SdKfz250 (1941) armored halftracks would provide some mobility for *panzergrenadier* mechanized infantry. The bulk of the German infantry would continue to move forward afoot, and most artillery and supply functions would remain horse-drawn until 1945. In October 1935 three *panzerdivisionen* were formed, but German armored doctrine was still not integrated into the greater German war doctrine.

# Italy

In theory Italian armored doctrine closely followed that of Germany, but the Italians were even more lacking in industrial infrastructure. They still constructed tanks by riveting armor plate onto internal frameworks, a practice abandoned by most countries.

Italian general doctrine reflected the Spanish Civil War experience, so deployment of artillery and antitank guns well forward with the infantry (*fuoco da manovra*, fire and maneuver) was emphasized. Tanks and the Semovente assault guns were very much seen as infantry support weapons, but the greatest failing was in the coordination with other arms. The Italians were avid followers of their own Guilio Douhet's concept of airpower as exclusively a strategic bombardment arm, and as a result Italy never developed true tactical support aviation.

# Japan

Japan was the next to squander the potential of the tank. Japan strove to establish itself as a world power, but lacked raw materials or industrial capacity. The Japanese had carefully observed the fighting in France, purchased a British Mark IV Female, and later many more Whippets, FTs, and advanced Renault NC27s. Tank enthusiasts were mostly junior officers, but by 1929 Japan created the prototype Type 89 I-Go medium tank. Senior officers expressed limited enthusiasm; contributing to the absence of a doctrine was the lack of a strong cavalry tradition, and a medieval mindset among senior officers. Infantry was considered the decisive arm, with a *bushido* emphasis on personal combat.

The I-Go was as advanced as any tank of its day, but Japanese development stagnated. Later Japanese tanks were thinly armored and under-gunned, scattered about as adjuncts to infantry formations, and seldom appearing in any strength above that of a company. Poor communications often led to uncoordinated attacks and tactical disasters.

The Japanese also fell into the trap of basing their tank and antitank weaponry on the capabilities of their own tanks. They discovered too late that many of their weapons, like the so-called tape-measure mine designed to break the tracks on a tank, did not even annoy the bigger American tanks. False conclusions were drawn from the fighting against the Soviets at Khalkhin Ghol in 1939, where about 80 percent of tank losses were to antitank guns. New antitank gun designs were rushed into production, but by 1943 Japanese guns could not penetrate American armor at any but suicidal ranges. The Japanese increasingly came to rely upon suicidal infantry assaults when faced with tanks. Few changes were made to fundamental tank designs or doctrine, and Allied troops described a consistent tendency to engage in attacks without infantry support, to aimlessly motor about the battlefield, or to sit immobile in defensive postures until destroyed.

# The Chinese Civil War and the Sino-Japanese Wars

China's first tanks were FTs abandoned after the 1919 Allied Vladivostok intervention, and a dozen more were purchased by warlord Zhang Zuolin. With the death of the only leader with any national status, Sun Yat-sen, in 1925 the Koumintang (KMT) under Chiang Kai-shek and their Communist allies parted ways. By 1937 the KMT had purchased more FTs and

*Japanese tank doctrine perceived the tank as strictly a direct infantry support weapon, and the Japanese never developed a true tank doctrine. Designs were primarily light vehicles like this Type 94 Ti-Ke "tankette," armed with a single machine gun. (NARA)*

various models from the British Vickers company.

In 1927 Soviet advisors were expelled by the KMT, replaced by Germans who encouraged purchase of tanks from Italy, England, and France as well as Panzer Is. The 1932 Manchurian Incident was a manufactured excuse for a Japanese invasion, and from then onward there were a series of battles against Japanese armor in China. In February 1933 the Japanese defeated Chinese forces at Rehe, but were unable to catch the retreating Chinese. An *ad hoc* mechanized column built around 11 I-Gos was not only able to successfully pursue but rout a large Chinese army in a surprise attack.

German support ended in July 1937 when Germany joined Japan in the Tripartite Pact (Axis). The Germans were replaced by Soviet advisors eager to counter Japanese expansionism, and they supplied T-26 tanks.

In the Second Sino-Japanese War the Japanese dispatched a tank brigade built around two tank battalions, but Major General Hideki Tojo dismantled the brigade to scatter its components around other units whose commanders had no idea how to use tanks. In the battle of Xinkou (October 1937) a battalion of light tanks was sent into a frontal assault on Chinese Central Army units armed with new German PaK 35/36 antitank guns, with disastrous result.

## Khalkhin Gol (Nomonhan)

In 1939 the Japanese finally overreached, and the Soviet Union and Japan fought an undeclared war. The Japanese Kwantung Army had grown into a semi-autonomous force, ignoring its own command structure and provoking the Soviets. On May 11, 1939 Manchurian and Mongolian cavalry clashed in the disputed zone, and the conflict escalated. The Japanese launched a major offensive with the intent of ousting the "invaders," with a formidable armored force consisting of the 3rd Tank Regiment (30 Type 89 and Type 97 medium tanks, and 11 Type 94 and

Type 97 tankettes) and the 4th Tank Regiment (36 Type 95 light tanks, eight Type 89 medium tanks, and four Type 94 tankettes).

The Soviets, under the leadership of Georgy Zhukov, encircled and virtually destroyed the main Japanese thrust, while the southern force suffered heavy losses at the hands of Soviet antitank guns. The Japanese reportedly lost 42 tanks and the Soviets 66 tanks, but Soviet losses were replaceable.

The stubborn Japanese launched another failed offensive from July 23–25, and Zhukov had had enough. He assembled a huge force that included the 4th, 6th and 11th Tank Brigades (500 or more tanks) and the 7th and 18th Mechanized Brigades with 400 or more armored cars plus infantry. The Japanese government had withdrawn its support for the rebellious Kwantung Army, who scrambled to counter the Soviet threat.

On August 20, Zhukov launched his offensive against the Japanese 23rd Infantry Division. Armor swept around both Japanese flanks, and Japanese counterattacks failed. Soviet losses were enormous, but Zhukov achieved his strategic goal of neutering the Kwantung Army so that Soviet assets could face a looming war with the Nazis without threats from the east.

Many of the Nomonhan lessons were never fully assimilated. Lessons absorbed by the Soviets were that gasoline engines were "a bit fire prone," and that closer tank–infantry coordination was needed. Khalkhin Ghol should have led the Japanese to re-examine tank designs and doctrine. The 45-mm guns of the Soviet tanks could penetrate the Japanese armor at long ranges, while the low-velocity Japanese guns were hopelessly outranged.

Tojo (appointed War Minister in 1940) and other senior officers seized upon the failures as justification for dismantling the armored units. Not until after seeing the results of the German *blitzkrieg* did the Japanese reconstitute large armored units, but by mid-1942 it was too late: Japanese designs were hopelessly outdated, and most industrial production capacity had been diverted to ships and aircraft.

# Testing Ground—the Spanish Civil War

Germany dispatched a total of 102 Panzer Is, and four Kleiner Panzer Befehlswagen I (a radio-equipped command tank) to Spain in September 1936, shortly after the outbreak of the war, to serve with Francisco Franco's Fascist forces as the Condor Legion. Other nations also rushed to test their military hardware at the expense of unhappy Spain: French FTs, Soviet BT-5s and T-26s, and one British-manufactured Vickers to the Popular Front, and Panzer Is and Italian tankettes to Franco's Nationalist Front.

The first significant tank action came on October 29, in a Republican attack on Sesena, south of Madrid. With no doctrine on how to use tanks, 15 T-26 tanks simply charged into the town. The infantry of the supporting 1st Mixed Brigade "had been moving well at first, but after 1,500 meters, they had felt tired and sat down." The tanks were forced to withdraw. The battle of Guadalajara (March 8–23, 1937) saw the first extensive test of Italian tanks. Nationalist forces were supposed to test the German *blitzkrieg* doctrine, but efforts bogged down in atrocious weather, poor reliability of Italian vehicles, and the superiority of the Republican T-26 tanks.

The Spanish experience largely provided opportunity for each side to test hardware. Due to the nature of the war few lessons were learned about military operations and doctrine. The Fascists exploited minor successes as propaganda victories, lending an air of invincibility to their armored operations. The war did see the relatively extensive use of improvised weapons like the "Molotov cocktail" antitank gasoline bomb. In one apocryphal incident a column of Nationalist tanks was thwarted by laying dinner plates upside-down in the road: the tank crews thought they were mines.

# CHAPTER 3

▓▓▓▓▓▓▓▓▓▓▓▓▓▓▓▓▓▓▓▓▓▓▓▓▓▓▓▓▓▓▓▓▓▓▓▓▓▓▓▓▓▓▓▓▓▓▓▓
▓▓▓▓▓▓▓▓▓▓▓▓▓▓▓▓▓▓▓▓▓▓▓▓▓▓▓▓▓▓▓▓▓▓▓▓▓▓▓▓▓▓▓▓▓▓▓▓

# WORLD WAR II

## War in Europe

IN 1939 GERMANY WAS LESS WELL prepared for war than now commonly assumed, and the prospect of war terrified many German generals. The bulk of the Wehrmacht was "leg infantry," the artillery horse drawn, there were far too few trucks, and the tank fleet numerically and technologically inferior. The only thing Germany had going for it was the doctrine of *blitzkrieg*.

The Western nations were even less prepared for war, and hastily reassembled armored forces that dated back to the Great War. Most French tanks were still perfectly serviceable designs, and remaining stocks of FTs were organized into light tank battalions, independent companies, and airfield defense detachments.

### *Poland, 1939*

The German-Soviet Pact of August 1939 assured that Poland would be dismembered, divided between Germany and the Soviet Union. The Nazis lost no time, invading Poland on September 1. German-Slovakian forces held a huge numerical

In 1938 Germany had bloodlessly annexed the Sudetenland region of **Czechoslovakia**. In addition to territory, Germany gained immense military stores, including Czechoslovakian LT vz 34 tanks, renamed Panzerkampfwagen 38(t) tanks, superior to German models.

advantage, with 63 divisions and six separate brigades versus 39 Polish divisions (several never fully mobilized) and 16 separate brigades, 2,750 tanks versus 880 for the Poles, and over 2,300 aircraft versus 400 Polish aircraft. Many of the Polish tanks, particularly the 7TP, were qualitatively superior to the German models. They were just too few and too uncoordinated. Even worse, the attack came from three sides.

The Nazi onslaught paralyzed the Polish civil government. The Poles staged a successful withdrawal of 20 divisions into a mountainous region, to hold out until French and British help could arrive. Then the Soviets attacked from the east in overwhelming force. The Poles were able to evacuate a major part of their forces through Romania, to form the Polish Armed Forces In The West, to fight bravely and well on behalf of England and France.

Modern analysts have concluded that despite the stunning success, the campaign was hardly a successful test of the *blitzkrieg* doctrine. *Panzer* units remained timid of threats to their flanks, and largely subordinate to the infantry and artillery. The successful Polish withdrawal belies the idea that swift and deep penetrations paralyzed the Polish military command structure, the basic goal of maneuver warfare.

## The Winter War

The Winter War between the Soviet Union and Finland (November 30, 1939–March 13, 1940) was fought primarily over control of the sea approaches to Leningrad. The Finns were hopelessly outnumbered (the Soviets had thrice the number of troops, and one hundred times as many tanks), but Soviet leadership had been gutted by purges. In a series of brutal battles the Finns inflicted 52 times as many casualties, and 120 times as many tanks destroyed. The result was a negotiated "interim peace." For the Soviets retrospection led to changes in leadership and equipment, which were not fully implemented before the summer of 1941.

## The Battle of France, 1940

Starved for raw materials, Germany invaded Denmark in April 1940 as a preliminary to invading Norway. Norway had no tanks or antitank weapons, so the armored force sent there consisted of Panzer Is and IIs, later augmented by three experimental heavy tanks after almost all the light tanks were lost when their transport was sunk by a British submarine. Opposed by 15 French H-39 light tanks, both sides used tanks in a limited infantry support role in the unsuccessful Allied attempt to defend Narvik.

The military and political collapse in the face of the 1940 German invasion of France and the Low Countries has obscured the fact that French tanks outclassed their German foes. In numerous encounters French tanks inflicted lopsided defeats. On May 16, the French and Germans were engaged in heavy fighting for the strategic village of Stonne, with several Chars B1 bis of the 3e Division Cuirassée pitted against the 10th Panzer Division. One tank under Captain Pierre Billotte led a counterattack, and took on several Panzer III and Panzer IV tanks. While 140 German shells bounced off Billotte's armor, he methodically destroyed two Panzer IVs, 11 Panzer IIIs, and two artillery pieces. German General Heinz Guderian wrote of another encounter:

> While the tank battle was in progress, I attempted, in vain, to destroy a Char B with a captured 47-mm antitank gun; all the shells I fired at it simply bounced harmlessly off its thick armor.

Our 37-mm and 20-mm guns were equally ineffective against this adversary. As a result, we inevitably suffered sadly heavy casualties.

Following the French capitulation the German Army happily accepted many of the best French tanks, though the French tanks were not particularly suited to German doctrine. Advanced vehicles like the S-35 and H35 were used in limited numbers on the Eastern Front, a few against the Allies in Normandy, but most were used for internal security and training. Despite the shock they had caused, the Germans were less enamored of the Char B1; most were used for training or converted to other uses.

## America Struggles to Catch Up

The collapse of France came as a shock to the United States Army, but the German *blitzkrieg* should not have come as such a shock. It was the consummation of the unfulfilled American armored warfare plan from the last war.

The stunning success of the *blitzkrieg* led to many false conclusions. American planners missed the primary lesson that the *panzer* units were combined-arms forces. It was assumed that all of Germany's forces were mechanized, and in the rush to emulate the German model the Americans created armored divisions that were too tank heavy, with eight tank battalions and only two infantry battalions. Also ignored were the facts that in *blitzkrieg* infantry created the breakthrough, the tanks exploited it. The greatest benefit was that the horse disappeared entirely from American planning. The Americans also grossly overestimated the capabilities of German tanks, and as an unintended consequence the United States would be given a jump on tank design, with 75-mm guns as the primary armament.

The Army belatedly formulated an actual tank doctrine. Training Circular Number 4 (September 1940) held that the armored division was a "self-sustaining unit of specially equipped elements of the combined arms and services." In recognition of its limitations, "It has great offensive power and mobility but only a limited and temporary capacity for the defense." Four months later a tentative field manual outlined the primary function of the tanks as that of seizing key objectives, envelopment, exploitation, and pursuit.

Formulation of doctrine required modern vehicles to execute it, but even with its huge capacity America could not keep pace with demand for tanks. The primary division weapon was the M2A4 light tank, fast and reliable but with a puny 37-mm main gun. The M2A1 medium tank was more heavily armored, but with the same turret and 37-mm main gun as the light tank, and with six machine guns in casemates, very much the "mobile pillbox" of older days. Recognition of the M2A1's limitations drove the design of the M3 medium tank with a 75-mm main gun. American industry could not yet manufacture the crucial race ring, the large toothed gear that allowed 360-degree traverse of the turret. The compromise was a limited-traverse 75-mm gun mounted on the right front of the huge box-like hull, and a 37-mm gun mounted in a small turret atop the tank.

In 1941 large-scale maneuvers by the U.S. Third Army experimented with the 1st Armored Division built around Adna R. Chaffee's 7th Mechanized Cavalry. The maneuvers demonstrated the ascendancy of the armored vehicle, but analysis led to a doctrinal dead end with long-lasting consequences because the rules were rigged. General Leslie McNair was in charge of the exercises, and was an advocate of the tank-destroyer concept of highly mobile antitank guns employing hit-and-run and ambush tactics. Self-propelled antitank guns, plus the infantry's organic towed antitank guns, would be deployed on the flanks of any enemy penetration to channel and destroy enemy tanks. Analysis of the maneuvers concluded that:

> armored forces are not invincible. On the contrary, the proper use
> of antitank weapons, terrain, and demolitions supplied the answer

*The M4 series of medium tanks was the backbone of the U.S. armored force in World War II. Produced in mass numbers, it was exported to all Allied countries. This M4A2 (the diesel-engine variant) is in use by the U.S. Marine Corps 1st Tank Battalion on Peleliu. (Grey Research Center)*

to the problem of meeting what had been described as the hardest and fastest striking force in modern warfare.

The new doctrine would be to organize a projected tank destroyer force of 220 separate battalions, at the expense of the tank force. Doctrine was changed to specify that tanks should not engage enemy tanks, but instead be held for offensive operations. The abundant M4 medium tanks eventually replaced the towed guns, guns on trucks or halftracks, and purpose-built tank destroyers like the M10 and M36 appeared. Ultimately 70 independent tank battalions became integral parts of infantry divisions, independent of the armored force. Two-thirds of all American tanks belonged to these separate battalions. A far-reaching consequence of the McNair doctrine was the delay in development and deployment of an American heavy tank until late 1944, and then only in limited numbers.

In August 1941 General Adna Chaffee died, replaced by Major General Jacob Devers. Devers set about reconciling American tank doctrine with European experience, plus some innovations. The proportion of medium to light tanks was increased, self-propelled artillery replaced towed guns, and light observation aircraft were made organic to the division. Devers' greatest innovation was the Combat Command, an independent headquarters staff to which division assets could be allocated to accomplish the mission at hand. The Combat Command had no fixed structure, but was task-oriented. In future wars the concept would be widely applied and become a fundamental concept of American military organization.

# War in the Pacific

American, British, and Commonwealth forces in Asia and the Pacific faced a war characterized by amphibious operations, hostile terrain, and an enemy who emphasized suicidal infantry antitank tactics. As a result the Allies developed differing tank doctrines, all of which emphasized close tank–infantry coordination.

Thanks to the patronage and insistent prodding of the Navy, the American Marine Corps was by 1941 arguably the service best-prepared for war. The Marine Corps had created the Advanced Base Force for the capture and defense of advanced naval bases, but had no coherent doctrine for doing so: operations like those in Mexico in 1914 were marked by improvisation. By 1918 the Navy had foreseen a coming war with expansionist Japan, and realized that any war plan involved a naval campaign with the capture of island naval bases by amphibious operations. The problem was that the Franco-British fiasco at Gallipoli (February 1915–January 1916) had convinced military theoreticians that firepower had rendered amphibious operations impossible. No one had informed the Japanese of this "fact," and faced with a different strategic problem, the Japanese continued to develop an amphibious capability, if not a coherent doctrine.

As the Marine Corps struggled to survive force reductions of the post-war era, they returned to the Advanced Base Force mission. After service in France and postwar expeditionary service, Major Earl H. "Pete" Ellis was assigned to develop an amphibious doctrine. Ellis threw himself into the task with superhuman zeal, and his staff soon published Operation Plan 712—*Advanced Base Operations in Micronesia*. This detailed manual for amphibious operations would profoundly affect the conduct of World War II, as it laid the foundation for amphibious landings from Guadalcanal to Normandy.

A basic tenet of the doctrine was to incorporate tanks into the landing force since naval gunfire was too inaccurate to reduce specific targets, but the Marines carried the concept little farther. Marine Corps officers were assigned to the Army tank school at Fort Knox, but in general only field-grade officers were placed in the tactical courses. Company-grade officers were assigned to tank maintenance courses.

The technical problems seemed insurmountable. Suitable tanks *and* landing boats had to be developed on a shoestring budget, so for two decades the Marine Corps struggled to integrate armor. One vehicle design by J. Walter Christie was a truly amphibious "tank" equipped with a cannon that fired through the front plate. By the late 1930s the Marines had settled upon a series of specially designed Marmon-Herrington tankettes, light enough to be lifted by a transport ship's boat cranes into a landing barge. The problem was that the armament—machine guns only—made the vehicle less than useful.

The solution came from boat designer Andrew J. Higgins, who on his own initiative designed the Landing Craft, Mechanized (LCM) capable of carrying a light tank. This allowed the Marines to adopt Army light tanks, but the problem now shifted from the technical back to the doctrinal. The Marine Corps division organization reflected a misinterpretation of the German mechanized division. With a large tank-destroyer contingent, mechanized reconnaissance company, and an unwieldy tank battalion with 72 light tanks plus scout cars, it was more suited to European warfare. The model for how the Marine Corps would conduct the coming war, if not the basic doctrine, was about to experience a profound shock.

When Japan attacked Pearl Harbor on December 7, 1941 it was but part of a cascade of Japanese expansionism. The Japanese perceived little need for armor in their campaigns of conquest, and still had no coherent armor doctrine. The primary Japanese armored thrusts were in the Philippines, into Malaya and Burma, with lesser operations in the Dutch East Indies, and Milne Bay on New Guinea.

The Japanese deployed the 4th and 7th Tank Regiments to the Philippines with 38 light tanks, and 14 light tanks and 34 medium tanks, respectively. They were faced with 108 American M3 light tanks of the 192nd and 194th Tank Battalions. American tanks were plagued by the usual doctrinal failures, since both the higher commanders and the tank unit leaders had no experience to suggest the importance of tank–infantry coordination. Though numerically and qualitatively superior, the American tank force was undone by logistical shortages and mechanical failures. There were no high-explosive or canister rounds for the 37-mm guns. The tanks' main guns had never been test fired, and when the crews test fired them just before battle, the recoiling cannon tubes jammed.

In their first clash with the Type 95 light tanks of the 4th Tank Regiment, the Americans could deploy only five tanks by draining all the others of fuel. On December 22, 1941, unsupported tanks from B Company, 192nd Tank Battalion, ran into a roadblock with enemy tanks, antitank guns, and infantry. The engagement demonstrated both the advantages and shortcomings of the M3 light tank. The radial aircraft engines were astonishingly tough: separate cylinder "jugs" could be shot away, and it just kept running. But the large vertical front hatches that opened to give the driver clear vision were vulnerable, and strikes that did not penetrate the armor sent rivets ricocheting around inside. One American tank was lost, the rest retreated.

In ensuing battles the tanks were hampered by poor communications, and infantry officers persisted in scattering tanks, often singly. The American tanks skirmished with the Japanese throughout the retreat into Bataan, where the M3s were ordered destroyed on April 9, 1942.

The unexpectedly stubborn American and Filipino resistance had thrown the Japanese timetable off, and two Type 97 Shinhoto Chi-Has, Japan's most modern tank, were rushed to Luzon. The Americans staged a last stand on Corregidor, and the Japanese landed the Type 97s and one captured M3 in the final assault.

The British regarded Singapore as impregnable to attack from the sea, but the Japanese staged landings on the Malay peninsula and attacked overland. They deployed three tank regiments, the 1st , 6th, and 14th, the two former including a total of 56 Shinhoto Chi-Has. In the struggle for Malaya the main fighting was accomplished by Japanese infantry infiltrating around the road-bound British forces. The Japanese devoted the 14th Armored Regiment to their Burma campaign, with four medium tank companies (Type 89 and Type 97s) and a light tank company (Type 95s). This force was augmented by one—possibly two—companies with light tanks and Type 94 tankettes.

The British were in the process of redeploying forces from North Africa to Malaya when Singapore fell on February 15, 1942. The force included most of the 7th Armoured Brigade: the 7th Queen's Own Hussars, and the 2nd Royal Tank Regiment. At first the primary tanks were American M3 light tanks, much valued for mechanical reliability. British Valentine infantry tanks were heavily armored, but the 2-pounder (40-mm) limited their utility.

The British tanks were expected to help hold against Japanese forces advancing from Thailand. Instead, the force was driven into the longest retreat in British military history. In the running battle of some 400 miles (650km) all the way back into India, neither side demonstrated any particular acumen at tank–infantry coordination. The long retreat, summarized in detail by Bryan Perrett in *Tank Tracks To Rangoon*, was a litany of incidents in which tanks had to launch attacks or fight their way out of Japanese traps, usually unsupported by infantry. For their part, the Japanese tanks were simply hapless. Perrett: "In spite of the severe lessons taught them by General Zhukov at Khalkhin-Gol during the 1939 Manchurian Incident, Japanese tank crews never gave the slightest hint that they were capable of fighting a tank battle, and in fact some of their ideas were downright peculiar."

The British tank crews also noted a shortcoming: the near total absence of communication and coordination between Japanese units. The retreat also exposed the shortcomings of Japanese antitank doctrine based on close assault by infantry. In a notable incident a Japanese officer leapt aboard a light tank and attacked the tank commander with a sword. The tank commander countered with the most available weapon—a hammer—and knocked the officer into the road. The tank tracks crushed his legs, but the enraged man continued to fire his pistol at the departing tank. The Burmese battles saw the first reported use of peculiarly Japanese weapons, among them the Frangible Smoke Grenade, a glass sphere filled with a chemical that produced an acrid smoke, intended to blind the tank crew.

The Japanese thrust into India was finally halted at the siege of the Admin Box, amid bitter fighting. The tanks provided direct-fire support to which the Japanese had no counter except suicidal bayonet charges.

## The Solomon Islands

As the Allies regained the initiative and switched over to offensive strategies following the naval victory at Midway, shortages of amphibious assault vessels, particularly those capable of landing heavy vehicles like tanks, would become an over-arching concern. In 1943 General George C. Marshall remarked that "Prior to the present war I never heard of landing craft except as a rubber boat. Now I think of little else." Winston Churchill wrote that "How is it that the plans of two great empires like Britain and the United States should be so hamstrung and limited by a hundred or so of these vessels [LSTs] will never be understood by history."

On August 8, 1942 two tanks from 3rd Platoon, C Company, 2nd Tank Battalion splashed ashore on the small island of

Tanambogo, where the landing force had been pinned down. The tanks advanced covered by infantry fire, but with no means of coordination the tanks drew too far ahead among the trees. Within a matter of seconds, both tanks were immobilized and swarmed by Japanese troops who killed or badly wounded the crewmembers.

The main landings on Guadalcanal were unopposed, but the jungle campaign that followed was marred by poor tank–infantry coordination and reckless actions by the tanks. In the pre-dawn hours of August 21, the Japanese tried unsuccessfully to force a crossing of the Ilu River. The next morning a platoon of tanks crossed the river and pursued the survivors into a coconut grove. There they swirled about machine-gunning, firing canister, and simply running over Japanese survivors until, as one observer noted, the rear plates and tracks were covered with blood, shreds of flesh, and splinters of bone. In contrast, on September 13 a platoon of tanks charged across an open field unsupported by infantry, and right into the sights of waiting antitank guns.

In the New Georgia campaign (June 30–October 7, 1943) the light tanks of the Marine Corps' 9th, 10th, and 11th Defense Battalions supported Army troops in a horrific jungle campaign, but the 37-mm guns of the light tanks proved inadequate to destroy Japanese fortifications. New Georgia did see a critically important innovation, the tank–infantry telephone—simply two field telephones, one in the turret and the other hung from the rear of the tank.

Because of limitations imposed by mountains and jungle, Army and Marine Corps tanks would play a less prominent role in the prolonged fighting on Bougainville (November 1, 1943–August

The **defense battalions** were heavy weapons units for advanced base defense, but were assigned to support Army divisions that lacked heavy weapons. They included a platoon of light tanks, antiaircraft guns, and heavy artillery.

21, 1945), and New Britain (December 15, 1943–August 21, 1945) campaigns to neutralize the Japanese base at Rabaul.

## The Southwest Pacific

After New Georgia, the Americans pursued a two-front strategy. Douglas MacArthur would skillfully bypass major centers of resistance, instead seizing sites for airfields to neutralize big Japanese bases like Rabaul. Because of conditions tanks were seldom employed in units larger than a platoon, and often as few as one or two tanks. Biak Island saw another of the few Japanese armored counterattacks when two Type 95 Ha-Gos charged three American M4A1 tanks. An American tank quickly demolished the trailing Ha-Go, trapping and then wrecking the lead tank. An American participant said that "the light Jap tanks looked like Volkswagens as contrasted to our medium General Sherman tanks that looked like monsters."

Admiral Nimitz, would follow a similar strategy in the Central and North Pacific, isolating Truk.

## The Central Pacific—the Gilbert Islands

Seizure of the two main atolls of the Gilbert Islands chain, Tarawa and Makin, would see a turning point in tank doctrine. In Hawaii two companies of the Army's 193rd Tank Battalion were re-equipped with M3 medium tanks. The battalion was attached to the 27th Infantry Division, but there was no time to train in coordinated tactics, and little doctrine existed for doing so. Rehearsal landings revealed a tendency for infantry to go to ground all over the beach, leaving the tanks no clear path ashore.

The Army landing plan for Butaritari Island on Makin Atoll was complex, with several widely separated landing beaches. Following the amphibious doctrine of the Marines, the light tanks would go ashore with the initial waves of infantry, with

*The problems of landing tanks in an amphibious assault led to the design of armed amphibians like this LVT(A)-1, an amphibian tractor with a modified M3 light tank turret, on the beach at Peleliu, late 1944. (U.S.M.C. History Division)*

medium tanks to follow. The light tanks headed for prearranged rally points, but then refused to take orders from infantry officers. The infantry moved rapidly ahead, and the tanks did not catch up until five hours after the landings. Fortunately the defenses on Butaritari were not very formidable, with no antitank defense except ditches.

The 27th Division's four-day-long reduction of the island was slow and systematic, and offshore the operational commander, Marine Major General Holland M. Smith fumed over the pace. Amphibious doctrine called for rapid subjugation of the enemy defenses in order to minimize the air and submarine threat to the transport ships offshore. Landing force casualties at Makin were very light—66 killed—but on November 24 the aircraft carrier *Liscombe Bay* was torpedoed with the loss of 644 crewmen.

The Japanese regional headquarters on Betio Island on the Tarawa Atoll was far more heavily fortified and garrisoned by Special Base Force and Special Naval Landing Force troops equipped with heavy guns and a tank detachment. The landings there would be the first true test of the amphibious assault doctrine, an attack on a heavily defended beach.

At the last moment the operational planners broke with their own doctrine of sending light tanks ashore with the first wave. Betio is subject to unpredictable seasonal low tides, so the first waves of infantry made it ashore in the new LVT tracked amphibian troop carriers, but the landing boats that followed hung up on the shallow reef edge hundreds of yards offshore. The careful landing plan degenerated into chaos. The remaining infantry waded ashore under heavy fire: casualties were extraordinarily heavy, and unit cohesion disappeared. Lieutenant Ed Bale's 14 medium tanks had no fording gear to negotiate the deeper water behind the reef edge. Several were lost falling into water-filled bomb craters. Light tanks, stuck by tons of material piled in cargo holds could not be landed the first day.

Once ashore the medium tanks faced a gauntlet of suicide attackers, enemy tanks, and guns of all calibers particularly the Japanese 75-mm Type 88 antiaircraft gun. The communications net broke down, leaving the surviving tanks to fight in isolation. There was no provision for communicating directly with the infantry, and the tactic of having the tank unit's own "recon guides" advance on foot ahead of the tanks to spot targets proved suicidal.

The landing came perilously close to failure, but the next morning Bale "ran into an infantry company commander [Major Mike Ryan]" and the two planned how to cooperate in a sweep down one beach. The impromptu tank–infantry team cleared a section of beach allowing reinforcements to come ashore as organized units, turning the tide of battle.

The Gilbert Islands battles were the subject of intense soul-searching, but there were clear indications that many senior officers still did not understand the flaws in existing tank doctrine. On Butaritari, Army tank officers noted the inability of infantry to communicate with tanks, and that, as described by Lieutenant James W. Lawrence: "Tanks were exposed dangerously by being sent too far ahead of the infantry. Had the enemy possessed antitank guns and other antitank weapons, we would have lost many tanks." One was a senior Marine Corps staff officer trained at Fort Knox who interrogated Bale: "One of the things he asked was 'Why didn't you cruise on the objective?' That was the term that was used for running around on the objective. That was a tactic that the Army taught. I don't know whether it came from the horse cavalry running over a hill and riding around on the hilltop, or what the hell it came from."

Another lesson was that light tanks were obsolete. When the light tanks finally got ashore on Betio, their 37-mm proved inadequate. Clearly medium tanks were needed, but industry was not producing enough of them to supply the needs of the Army and the Lend-Lease programs to the Allies. The Pacific would have to wait.

## The Marshall Islands

The huge Kwajelein Atoll was the next major stepping stone. Roi and Namur proved to be relatively lightly defended, but the lessons of other battles had not been fully absorbed by the inexperienced 4th Marine Division. Several light tanks, including a company commander's tank, were isolated and lost to close assault by Japanese infantry. Faced with no effective opposition, the medium tanks raced ahead of the infantry and into potential impact areas of heavy naval gunfire.

The Army's 7th Infantry Division and 767th Tank Battalion (equipped with M4A1 medium tanks) had better absorbed the lessons of the Gilberts. All tanks received telephone boxes fitted to the rear to communicate with infantry. The 767th also brought in M10 Tank Destroyers, which proved unsuited for the Pacific theater with a gun designed to fight other tanks and an open turret top, vulnerable to enemy swarming. The effectiveness of man-pack flamethrowers had been proven on Betio, but casualties among users were high. A few of the light tanks were fitted with flamethrowers in place of the bow machine gun but the range was pitifully short.

# The Mariana Islands

As the Central Pacific Drive entered the Mariana Islands, American tank doctrine shifted to another phase. Tanks remained very much an infantry support weapon, and the two components better understood each other's strengths and limitations. Captain Ed Bale remembered:

> There was a great effort to take tanks up to the infantry battalions and educate the infantrymen, to train them how to spot and call for fire, and how to protect the tanks from Japanese trying to swarm them and place mines on them. It was a mutual support proposition.

Army tank battalions continued to operate a mix of medium and light tanks. In Marine tank battalions the light tanks had been organized into a fourth "Dog Company" of old M3s converted to Satan flame tanks, with newer M5A1 light tanks as escorts. Tank–infantry teams could now shift seamlessly between tanks leading the way, protected by long-range infantry fire in open terrain, to infantry advancing first, covered by following tanks in densely vegetated or built-up areas.

Saipan saw the largest tank battle of the Pacific war, when the Japanese 9th Tank Regiment with advanced Type 97-kai Shinhoto Chi-Ha tanks and the 136th Infantry Regiment counterattacked on the evening of June 16, 1944. The Marines were equipped with bazookas, and supported by a company of M4A2 tanks and several tank destroyers. In a "madhouse of noise, tracers, and flashing lights" the Japanese were repulsed with the loss of 32 tanks and over 700 infantry.

In contrast, the Army 766th Tank Battalion attached to the 27th Infantry Division saw operations marred when tanks were sent unsupported into enemy-held ground, often with disastrous results. The 706th Tank Battalion trained extensively with the 77th Infantry Division for the assault on Guam. The 706th operated in larger increments, sending up to a company of 14 tanks with infantry support on armed reconnaissance operations, and cooperated fairly seamlessly with adjacent Marine Corps units.

## The Palau Islands

Between September 17 and September 20 the Army's 81st Infantry Division supported by the 710th Tank Battalion were able to seize Angaur Island against relatively light opposition. Nearby Peleliu was an entirely different proposition. The fighting there (September 15–November 27, 1944) was a period of transition for both the Americans and Japanese, as the Japanese shifted from a doctrine of counterattacks to one of forcing the Americans to root defenders out of pillboxes and interconnected cave complexes.

The Marine 1st Tank Battalion had deployed to Peleliu with only two companies as the result of a shortage of transport ships, and was quickly depleted by brutal fighting in the Umurbrogel hill complex. They were later relieved by the Army's 710th Tank Battalion.

## Return to the Philippines

The landings on Leyte provided an opportunity—or excuse—to return to the tank doctrine for large land masses. In a typical action on October 23, 1944, the experienced 767th Tank Battalion launched a battalion-scale "Flying Wedge" attack, leaving the infantry of the 17th Regiment, 7th Infantry Division to keep up as best they could. The column lost a number of tanks to mines and satchel charges, and officers to snipers. The tanks reached their first objective, but without infantry could not hold the town of Buraean. The next day the tanks moved ahead again and reentered the town, but found the streets impassable.

Infantry was necessary to clear the town, but once past the town the tanks were forced back by mines and swampy terrain. Once more tank–infantry teams, with infantry often riding the tanks, proved more successful in clearing towns and ambushes.

The problematic doctrinal issue here was that tanks units were sometimes "attached to" infantry units, and so subject to the infantry officers' orders, as opposed to acting "in support." Infantry officers were unfamiliar with the tanks' logistical needs, and would not release them for necessary replenishment of fuel and ammunition.

On the main island of Luzon, the Army tankers encountered outclassed Japanese tanks, but suffered losses to suicide attacks and antitank guns. At close ranges the 47-mm Japanese tank guns could be effective, and in an ambush on January 17, 1945, the 716th Battalion lost two M4s to an ambush before a third, damaged, tank was able to destroy or drive off the enemy tanks. In the final stages, including the capture of Manila, tank–infantry coordination was considerably improved.

## The Volcano Islands

The iconic battle for Iwo Jima (February 19–March 26, 1945) marked a full transition to a Japanese war strategy of attrition, fighting battles they knew they could not win. The battle saw the Marines improvising new tactics, the "corkscrew and blowtorch." A tank would pour suppressive fire onto a position, flamethrower men or flame tanks would burn it out, and engineers would blow it apart with explosive charges to prevent it being reoccupied through tunnels. Tanks equipped with dozer blades covered bunkers with rock and sand, burying the occupants alive.

Iwo Jima also saw the first widespread Japanese use of improvised mines, aircraft bombs, or torpedo warheads with antitank mines as detonators. These devices could lift a 30-ton tank high into the air, ripping it to pieces, and survivors were rare. It was perhaps the most ruthless battle of the Pacific War, a simple orgy of killing.

# Okinawa

The last battle of the Pacific War was a joint U.S. Army–Marine Corps operation with a huge armored force. Fifty-four Army M4 tanks of the 713th Tank Battalion (Flamethrower) supported seven "gun tank" battalions and were integrated at the platoon level.

On April 1, a handful of Army and Marine Corps tanks landed using the experimental T-6 flotation system, large steel pontoons attached to the tank by explosive bolts. The pontoons and propulsion by paddling tracks made the tank slow and almost impossible to steer.

The Japanese declined to defend the beaches, instead withdrawing inland. The Americans rapidly cleared the northern end of the island, often using combined-arms patrols. Bob Botts, Company A, 6th Marine Tank Battalion described that:

> We would take a bulldozer tank and three regular tanks and all the infantry we could pile on the four of them. We'd just take off down the road until we ran into something.

Most of the Japanese had withdrawn into the Shuri Line fortifications to the south. In a battle of attrition the tendency of the Japanese to reoccupy positions led to another shift in tactics, "processing." Tank–infantry teams would clear an area and withdraw, deliberately allowing the Japanese to reoccupy the now-known positions, and then do it all over again the next day. It was killing for the sheer sake of killing to deal with an enemy who would accept neither defeat nor mercy.

The lessons of prior battles had not been learnt by everyone. On April 19, the Army's Company A (Reinforced), 193rd Tank Battalion, unaccompanied by infantry, was assigned to move around the end of rugged Kakazu Ridge through Japanese-held ground and meet attacking infantry on the other side. The tanks got lost in a maze of trails, and were attacked by infantry and guns of the 22nd Independent Antitank Battalion. Of 30 tanks, 14 were lost and many of the crewmen killed.

In the Father's Day Massacre several tanks were lost and the only thing that saved many of the crewmen was the incredible toughness of the M4A2. The twin engines meant the tank could remain in action even when one engine was destroyed, and diesel fuel did not easily catch fire: several tanks retreated with smoking fuel sloshing to and fro in the crew compartment.

Terrain, new Japanese tactics, and sheer numbers made Okinawa the most costly campaign of the Pacific War for tank forces. It was a deadly portent of the price to be paid for any invasion of the Japanese Home Islands.

## The Burma–India Theater

The long retreat of 1942 taught the British harsh lessons about the necessity for infantry support, and the Bombay Grenadiers were assigned as special support infantry:

> They relieved [the 150th Regiment, Royal Armored Corps] of all its worries as to the safety of its tanks, acted as eyes in spotting targets, came with it where other infantry hesitated to follow, and accepted casualties in safeguarding their charges …

This new tank–infantry team would prove particularly important since a global shortage of landing craft forced a British land counteroffensive to recapture Burma, rather than a more effective amphibious operation to sever Japanese supply lines.

The tank considered the best in Burma was the obsolescent American M3 medium, and the design features that limited its utility in most theaters of war were considered advantages. The limited traverse of the hull-mounted 75-mm main gun was not generally considered an issue, and the gun's high-explosive shell was invaluable in dealing with Japanese fortifications. The small 37-mm turret gun fired a canister shell useful for blasting away at hidden snipers, and slaughtering suicidal Japanese infantry. The last tank to appear in Burma was the M4, several models of which saw service there. For their part the Japanese had developed improved ambush tactics to take advantage of the M3's limitations, which forced it to face the enemy head-on to bring its main gun to bear, exposing its rear to attack. The British also encountered a unique type of command-detonated antitank mine: a Japanese soldier crouched in a camouflaged hole in the road, with an aircraft bomb and a hammer to detonate it.

In summation, the Allied forces were driven by necessity to develop new tank–infantry doctrines, but each response was different. The U.S. Army was hampered by centralized school training, much of which was not applicable in the Pacific. The British adopted a model of assigning specialist infantry to protect tanks. The most effective doctrine, adopted by the U.S. Marines and several Army divisions was to train all infantry in close support of tanks.

## North Africa

When Mussolini foolishly tied Italy's fortunes to Hitler, it resulted in war along the border between Italian Libya and British Egypt. The British Eighth Army had things its own way until the arrival of German armored forces in March 1941. The war in North Africa would thenceforth be inextricably tied to one dominant personality—Erwin Rommel.

The North African experience is the classic example of the importance of coherent doctrine: British tank doctrine remained fundamentally flawed. Tanks were still divided into two roles, infantry tanks and cruiser tanks. Infantry tanks like the Matilda and Churchill were heavily armored, but often under-gunned. Cruiser tanks were intended as exploitation weapons, and the emphasis for designs like the Crusader was on speed at the expense of firepower and armor. Tanks were either dispersed attached to infantry formations (infantry tanks), or concentrated in small armored brigades (cruisers) with inadequate infantry support, and so the British advantage of numerical superiority was frittered away. In contrast, German doctrine emphasized concentration of armored force at the *schwerpunkt*, in military parlance the point of decision. German Lieutenant General Fritz Bayerlein summed up the British problem:

> Contrary to the principle that one can never be strong enough at the center of gravity and must concentrate everything at that point, every attack was made by part of only the Eighth Army, and even the main offensive force, already too weak for its purpose, was thrown into battle dispersed.

Frank Messervy of the 7th Armored Division, the "Desert Rats," concurred:

> His [Rommel's] handling of armour, anti-tank guns and mechanized formations in cooperation was, with the shwerpunkt idea, much better than our rather dispersed idea of fighting… We were given area commands, not functional commands—which kept fluctuating. We never fought as a division…

Messervy's reference to area versus functional commands pointed out another fundamental doctrinal flaw all too common in many armies. An area command refers to the promulgation of a very objective-specific orders (capture X physical objective), versus a functional order (destroy the enemy by any means necessary).

The Germans also proved more tactically innovative. A favored German tactic was for their armor to engage British tanks, then turn to flee. The pursuing British tanks would be lured onto a line of waiting antitank guns, from small weapons up to the famed 88s. By late 1942 the British had learned many harsh tactical and doctrinal lessons, and assigned larger contingents of infantry to cooperate with armored formations. The arrival of American-made M3 medium tanks was also a boon to Eighth Army. The 75-mm gun outranged many of the German antitank guns, and a counter-tactic to the gun line was to shell German

*Although North Africa is remembered for its armored battles, most of the forces were infantry. Erwin Rommel was a proponent of leading from the front to better control a rapidly evolving situation. (NARA)*

antitank guns from out of the enemy guns' range.

Lost in our modern perceptions of the North African battles is the fundamental fact that conditions were so harsh on mechanical equipment, and the numbers of tanks so limited, that at the conclusion of many battles the opposing armored forces were reduced to as few as ten or so functional tanks, and the decisive fighting was done by infantry.

New leadership in the Eighth Army in the person of General Bernard Montgomery eventually reversed British fortunes. Montgomery was a master of the set-piece battle. Taking advantage of superior Allied resources, Montgomery was patient enough to wait until he could overwhelm Rommel with superior resources, including the new M4 medium tanks, now flowing from America. The second battle of El Alamein (October 23–November 11, 1942) was the watershed of the North African war, and from that point Rommel would remain on the strategic defensive.

After America's entry into the war, the U.S. Army sent observers to serve with the British in North Africa. Unfortunately, neither American officers nor enlisted men held the British in very high regard, and crucial lessons went unheeded.

Operation *Torch*, the November 1942 invasion of Vichy French Morocco and Algeria, was the first experience of the American Army in amphibious warfare, and saw the first combat experience of American armor. The 1st and 2nd Armored Divisions were opposed by French FTs, no match for the American tanks. The Torch landings placed German forces in a perilous position, trapped between the victors of El Alamein in the east and the new Allied army in the west. The solution was a series of spoiling attacks designed to eliminate the western forces before Montgomery could develop logistical stockpiles to resume his offensive.

At the battle of the Faid Pass, American enthusiasm unconstrained by experience proved disastrous. Free French artillery created considerable carnage among the Germans, who then began to retreat with the American armor in pursuit. It was the usual German tactical trap, and an American artillery observer reported that:

> It was murder. They rolled right into the muzzles of the concealed eighty-eights and all I could do was stand by [his radio was disabled] and watch tank after tank blown to bits or burst into flames or just stop, wrecked.

In mid-February the Germans launched another attack directed at the Allied supply center of Sidi bou Zid. The onslaught drove the Allies back, with heavy losses in tanks and vehicles.

The first major test for the Americans was the battle of Kasserine Pass. On February 21 and 22, Rommel battered at Allied forces blocking the pass. American losses were appalling, but the attack was eventually contained, and losses to Allied artillery and reinforcements forced Rommel to break off his offensive. The Kasserine debacle demonstrated the inadequacy of American training, tactics, and doctrine, particularly a tendency to occupy defensive positions that were not mutually supporting.

The American experience in North Africa also marked the first

*In contrast to Rommel, British General (later Field Marshal) Bernard Montgomery was the master of the set-piece battle, using superior logistics and overwhelming power. (NARA)*

(and as it turned out, only) tests of the cherished tank-destroyer doctrine. At the Kasserine Pass, tank destroyers had proven effective when used according to doctrine, to hold the shoulders of an enemy penetration, bleed and contain the enemy, and lay the basis for a counterattack. Following the Kasserine Pass debacle George Patton assumed command of II Corps, and began an offensive toward the eastern Atlas Mountains. In the battle of El Guettar an attack by the 10th Panzer Division penetrated deeply enough to threaten the headquarters of the American 1st Infantry Division. Major General Terry Allen rebuffed suggestions to retreat: "I will like hell pull out, and I'll shoot the first bastard who does." The German offensive stalled and was set upon by American artillery, towed antitank guns, and M-10 tank destroyers. Within an hour over 30 German tanks were lost, their supporting infantry decimated.

The North African experience brought about changes in armor doctrine, which the Americans were now improvising on the fly. Rommel acknowledged the American doctrinal flexibility:

What was astonishing was the speed with which the Americans adapted themselves to modern warfare. In this they were assisted by their extraordinary sense for the practical and material and by their complete lack of regard for tradition and worthless theories… The organization, training, and equipment of the U.S. Army all bear witness to great imagination and foresight…

Henceforth the armored division's combat commands would be centrally controlled and coordinated at division level, rather than operating semi-autonomously. Patton simply ignored excessively detailed objective-specific orders issued by his superiors, promulgating his own functional orders as the situation unfolded. Exactly how these seemingly contradictory measures would coalesce into a coherent doctrine remained to be seen.

The Americans first encountered the German Tiger I heavy tank in North Africa, but resolutely stuck to the doctrine that tanks did not fight tanks. Improved coordination with artillery and air support was seen as a partial solution, but the net effect was to further delay the deployment of an American heavy tank.

American leaders recognized poor coordination with artillery and infantry, a persistent tendency to employ armor piecemeal, and the failure to concentrate forces at the *schwerpunkt*. Tactical failures were also apparent, among them poor reconnaissance. At the Kasserine Pass, when Combat Command C (1st Armored Division) moved forward to assist the badly damaged Combat Command A, they did so with no forward reconnaissance. The unsuspecting lead tank battalion ran head-on into two *panzer* divisions and was virtually annihilated.

For the remainder of the North African campaign the Axis forces would be squeezed into a shrinking perimeter around Tunis by Montgomery's systematic advance from the east, and the somewhat more extemporized American advance from the west. On May 13, 1943, the last Axis forces in North Africa surrendered.

Testifying to the accuracy of Rommel's analysis of American methodology, important lessons were quickly incorporated. Armored divisions were reduced to a more manageable size, and reorganized with fewer tanks and to include three battalions of infantry as opposed to one. The reorganization meant that the division could easily be subdivided into smaller combined-arms teams. Light tanks were relegated to the reconnaissance role. Logistical support was added at battalion level to make each self-sufficient.

## The Dieppe Rehearsal

On August 19, 1942, the British undertook a raid on the French port of Dieppe with some 6,000 men (largely Canadian) supported by Churchill Infantry tanks of the Calgary Regiment, 1st Canadian Tank Brigade. Designed to test amphibious doctrine, the feasibility of taking and holding a port (albeit for a short time), and to boost flagging Allied morale, it was an unmitigated disaster. Of 27 tanks landed, only three managed to get off the beach. Less than ten hours later the Allied troops withdrew, having lost 3,367 men.

Despite insistence that lessons learned at Dieppe were applied in Normandy, all that the British high command had really gained was the knowledge that the Western Allies were far from opening a Western Front to aid the hard-pressed Soviets, and that the Allies in Europe had much to learn about amphibious warfare.

## Sicily and the Italian Campaign

The Sicilian campaign was designed to be the first step in Churchill's beloved attack on the "soft underbelly of Europe" and would go far toward opening Allied sea lanes across the Mediterranean. On July 10, 1943, Allied landings put ashore the British Eighth Army in the east, the American Seventh Army in the west. The plan was for the main thrust to be Eighth Army sweeping up the east coast, across the very narrow coastal plain below Mount Aetna to capture the strategic port at Messina near Sicily's northeastern tip.

Predictably, Eighth Army became embroiled in a slow slog across the river plains south of Mount Aetna, and the port of Catania was finally captured at great cost on August 5. Meanwhile the mercurial Patton seized the opportunity to apply American (and British) armored doctrine as it should be, pushing the Americans north through lesser Axis resistance in the rugged interior mountains, then east along the northern coast. On August 1 Patton recorded that "The mountains are the worst I have ever seen. It is a miracle that our men can get through them but we must keep up our steady pressure. The enemy simply can't stand it, besides we must beat the Eighth Army to Messina."

The American effort along the north coast required crossing numerous river mouths, so the effort was largely conducted by infantry, but was an extension of the exploitation doctrine driven at a furious pace. The Americans, although covering a much longer and more tortuous route, on August 17 at about 1030 hours officially captured Messina, pulling into the central square minutes ahead of the British tanks.

# Western Europe—The Normandy Landings

The amphibious doctrine developed by the U.S. Marine Corps had been essentially swallowed whole by the U.S. Army, including the necessity of landing tanks. On the issue of how to get tanks ashore, the two parted ways. The Marines had long since adopted the LCM (Landing Craft, Mechanized) capable of carrying one medium tank directly onto the beach. The Army instead opted to use the British-designed Duplex Drive (DD) tank system. Marines who saw demonstrations were horrified. The rig offered a unique combination of low speed, poor maneuverability, extremely poor sea-keeping qualities, and vulnerability to enemy fire.

Three American, four British, and two Canadian tank battalions were to launch a first wave of DD tanks. The balance of the battalions would be landed directly onto the beach by landing craft. On the morning of June 6, 1944, the waves off the Normandy beaches were running up to 6 feet/1.83 m. Off most beaches the tanks were launched too far out, but by a miracle most made it to the beach. Their slow speed meant that many arrived after the engineer tanks following in heavy landing craft. Many could not identify navigational landmarks, while others were carried parallel to the beach by strong currents and landed in the wrong positions. Off Omaha Beach sea conditions were worst, and the American 741st Tank Battalion lost all but two of the 29 tanks they put into the water.

Once ashore, the differing Allied tank doctrines began to be felt. American doctrine maintained that tanks did not fight tanks. As a consequence the mass-produced M4 series, although increasingly inferior to the latest generation of German tanks, remained the backbone of American armored forces and the M4 was becoming the standard tank of the British and Free French. In the fighting in Normandy the need for a tank-killing machine to protect the 75-mm gun tanks was belatedly recognized. The British response was M4 "Fireflies" (tanks modified by the British to carry their 17-pounder gun), and the Americans produced 76-mm gun tanks in relatively small numbers. In both cases the usual doctrinal practice was to integrate the new tanks with 75-mm gun tanks at the company level. Increasing Allied airpower was seen as the better support for the armored force, but air–ground communications remained clumsy.

British doctrine remained essentially unchanged, though organizational changes were made. Armored divisions were reorganized to form a "tank heavy" armored brigade with three tank battalions and one infantry "motor battalion," and an infantry brigade of three battalions. A reconnaissance regiment included a tank battalion. The doctrinal problem that continued to bedevil the British was that they had no equivalent to the combat command/*kampfgruppe* structure. The two brigades were typically deployed as separate maneuver elements, with

*Massive production enabled the Americans to divert M4 tank production to specialized vehicles like this M32 tank recovery vehicle. (NARA)*

the motor battalion as a follow-on force to the tank battalions. As a result the tanks quite often received inadequate direct infantry support by German or American standards, though improvements were slowly implemented.

German overall doctrine was now the *vernichtungsslacht* ("destruction," or battle of annihilation), an outdated strategy of attrition. In this doctrinal model qualitative superiority in weapons would have to atone for numerical inferiority. This doctrine led to increased emphasis on specialized tank-killing tanks like the Panther, Tiger, and later models of the venerable Panzer IV.

By far the greatest doctrinal failure for the Germans was industrial. German production practices resulted in chronic shortages of spare parts, and it was common for a soldier at the front to be given home leave along with a list of spare parts to bring back to his unit. Mechanical complexity and poor reliability was a significant problem for German armored units. Photos exist of Panthers going into battle with a spare transmission strapped to the engine deck, and more Tigers were lost when they were abandoned than were lost to Allied action.

By mid-1944 the "paper strength" of a *panzer* division was

four infantry battalions and two tank battalions, with the ratio being six-to-two in SS *panzer* divisions. German divisions were nominally larger in manpower, 15,000–21,000 men as opposed to 11,000 for an American armored division and 15,000 for a British division. The difference was that the German division included logistical, air defense, and many other functions vested at corps or higher level in Allied forces. Not too much should be made of these numerical discrepancies. German units were always grossly understrength due to casualties and national manpower shortages, and often vehicle allocations were as low as 10 percent of the nominal strength.

# Caen—Purgatory of Commonwealth Armor

The city of Caen was a first-day objective for the British 3rd Infantry Division, but they fell 4 miles/6 km short of their objective. The failure led to a prolonged and bloody struggle for the city, which contained a crucial spoke-like road nexus and critical heavy-capacity bridges over the River Orne and the Canal de Caen à la Mer. The Germans rushed in units like the Panzer Lehr, 12 SS Panzer, and 21 SS Panzer. The concentration of *panzers* may seem odd for a defensive battle, but German SS *panzer* divisions were "infantry heavy."

The fighting was a series of nine named British offensives (*Perch*, the battle of Le Mesnil-Patry, *Martlet*, *Epsom*, *Windsor*, *Charnwood*, *Jupiter*, *Atlantic*, and *Goodwood*) in which the 7th Armoured Division and a variety of Canadian units played a repetitive role. A series of battles resulted only in stalemate, in part because the divisional brigades operated separately, and the tank-heavy brigade was often supported by unfamiliar infantry from other divisions.

Operation *Perch* was a rebuffed attempt to exploit a gap that had developed in the German positions, notable mainly for the questionable achievements of German Waffen-SS "tank ace" Michael Wittmann in the fighting for Villers-Bocage on June

13. An advancing British force surprised the Tiger I tanks of Wittmann's 2 Kompanie, schwere SS-Panzer Abteilung 101 near the town. Wittmann counterattacked, in turn surprising a British column that had halted for a command conference. Wittmann's force destroyed the column in a matter of minutes and continued into the town, where his tank was disabled. Wittmann managed to summon additional forces, and heavy fighting ensued. Tigers advanced into the town in a failed attempt to intimidate the British defenders. Several were destroyed by Fireflies, antitank guns, and even the infantry's PIAT grenade launchers. In one engagement worthy of Hollywood, a passing Firefly spotted a Tiger in ambush position on an adjacent street and fired through several open windows, disabling the enemy's gun. When the Tiger reversed course to withdraw, a British Cromwell raced out into the street behind it, fired once into the Tiger's exposed engine, and raced out of harm's way. Eventually the British commander decided the town was untenable without infantry, and withdrew.

Now much romanticized, Wittmann's feat was a creation of the Nazi propaganda apparatus. Nazi Germany's failing fortunes needed heroes. Wittmann was credited with *all* the British losses—14 or more tanks, two antitank guns, and 13–15 other vehicles.

*Jupiter* on July 10 was an attack by the 43rd Infantry Division and 4th Armoured Brigade on several villages and to push the Germans off Hill 112 southwest of Caen. The Germans were determined to hold the position, and committed five infantry battalions, two Tiger tank battalions, two assault gun companies, and rocket artillery. Both sides battled each other to a standstill, and the hill remained a no-man's land.

*Atlantic* was another bloody debacle, a failed attempt to push the Germans off the Verrières Ridge north of Caen, but the British were pushed back past their starting line. *Goodwood* was a massive attack with three armored divisions and a massive air bombardment that finally pushed German forces south of Caen. The massive bloodlettings around Caen had not been in vain, forcing Rommel to commit his *panzers* to a defensive battle, with no strategic reserve.

# Americans in the *bocage*

At first the American armored divisions played no decisive role since the opposing armies were entangled in the *bocage*, or hedgerow country. It was ideal for murderous ambush tactics by the heavily armored Panther and Tiger tanks, and the thinly armored M4s had to confront them head-on. It was also ideal for small-unit infantry defense: any unit breaking through a hedgerow found itself in a box exposed to fire from other hedgerows bounding the field. The fighting conditions cried out for the close-range firepower of the independent tank battalions, but tanks could not break through the dense root walls and tangled vegetation.

A solution came in the Culin (often misspelled Cullen) Cutter, a plow-like device manufactured from the steel of old German beach obstacles and fitted to the front of a tank. Sergeant Curtis G. Culin III of the 2nd Armored Division got the idea from another enlisted man, and sought in vain to credit the idea to him. It was another example of the American improvisation that had so impressed Rommel.

Operation *Cobra* commenced with a massive July 25 air bombardment designed to punch a hole through German defenses. The Americans had learned about the *schwerpunkt*, and by July 31 the Americans had broken through and were racing into open country. The only possible counter would have been the *panzer* divisions, but they had been bled white around Caen. Hitler ordered a counterattack, but among them the 2 Panzer, and the 1 and 2 SS Panzer Divisions could muster only 145 tanks and 24 *sturmgeschutz*.

The Normandy breakout was precisely the kind of action American armored doctrine emphasized. Disregarding flank security, combat commands slashed through or bypassed German resistance. The rapid pace was permitted by the mechanical reliability of the M4 and the flexibility of command structures: no orders were needed except the functional one of "go get the enemy." Soon Allied formations had all but encircled the German 5 Panzer and 7 Armies. Omar Bradley, now commander of the American 1st and 3rd Armies: "This is an opportunity that comes to a commander not more than once in a century. We're about to destroy an entire hostile army and go all the way from here to the German border." The U.S. 90th Infantry Division and Polish 1st Armoured Division finally closed the jaws on the trapped Germans. The Poles were wreaking revenge. Inside the Falaise Pocket, Allied fighters bombers strafed and rocketed packed German columns. The Germans left behind over 10,000

The **DD tank** hull was fitted with a boat-shaped canvas screen raised by pneumatic tubes. The screen displaced enough water that the tank floated with its turret top roughly at water level. In theory the freeboard (height of the sides above water level) was 3 feet/0.91 m, in practice less, and 1 foot/0.3 m waves were considered safe for navigation. Propulsion was by propellers geared to engage teeth on special rear idler wheels. The tank commander stood atop the turret and steered with rudders attached by lines to a tiller.

General Sir Percy Hobart of the 79th Armored Division devised an array of specialized vehicles, most based on Churchill tanks made redundant by the adoption of the American M4. Known as **"Hobart's Funnies"**, these included the Crab flail tank that detonated mines by beating the ground with heavy chains attached to a rotating drum, the Crocodile mechanized flamethrower, the Armored Vehicle Royal Engineer tank with a 290-mm mortar for destroying concrete positions, the Bobbin that laid a roll of reinforced matting to make soft ground traversable by tanks, a fascine carrier to fill antitank ditches, and the Small Box Girder and Ark bridging vehicles. All would prove to have a more lasting impact than the DD tanks.

dead, and 50,000 prisoners, as well as hundreds of tanks. The survivors fled toward the Seine with the Allies on their heels.

Allied generals hoped to avoid the potential delay and destruction involved in taking Paris, but a Resistance uprising began on August 19, and the French 2e Division Blindée and American 4th Infantry Division were diverted to secure the city.

In the end, the Allied advance raced some 450 miles/750 km, but was brought up short just before the German border by its own success. As supply lines became longer, fuel could not be moved forward fast enough. The pursuit ground to a halt and the Germans were granted a reprieve.

# The Great Allied Gamble—*Market Garden*

There ensued a struggle over who should be given priority of supplies for a renewed offensive, Montgomery or Patton. Field Marshal Montgomery was eventually given priority to execute *Market Garden*, a risky plan to penetrate deeply into German-held territory, seize bridgeheads over several rivers; the ultimate goal was the bridge over the Rhine River. If successful the offensive would open the way into Germany's Ruhr industrial heartland and quickly end the war.

*Market* would drop Allied airborne forces to capture and hold bridges. In *Garden* the British XXX Corps, spearheaded by armor, would race down a single narrow highway in a bold stroke to relieve the airborne forces. A glaring problem was that airborne forces had weak antitank capabilities, and would be terribly exposed for days. The bold plan was quite out of character

 **Assault guns** or ***Sturmgeschutz*** were self-propelled artillery built on tank chassis but with thicker armor and heavier guns that could only fire forward. They were intended to support infantry in the attack, but were an effective ambush weapon.

*Typical American tank doctrine was for tanks to lead the way in open terrain, with infantry providing covering fire from the rear. In dense vegetation or towns, infantry led the way with tanks providing supporting fire. These troops from the 55th Armored Infantry Battalion and the 22nd Tank Battalion are entering Wernberg, Germany, in April 1945. (NARA)*

for Montgomery, the master of the meticulously planned set-piece offensive. Although *Garden* would be spearheaded by armor, it was not consistent with either British or American armor doctrine. It could not be a fluid exploitation attack, but a prolonged frontal assault over 60 miles/97 km of two-lane road, much of it through terrain otherwise impassable to vehicles.

Things began to go awry shortly after the September 17 airdrops. XXX Corps met early and strong resistance, and airborne forces failed to capture certain bridges. XXX Corps was spearheaded by tanks and infantry, and despite heavy artillery support and waves of Allied fighter-bombers, the single-file advance began to falter on the first day. The plan was for the tanks to advance 13 miles/21 km. They achieved half that.

The advance of XXX Corps was slowed when German infantry formed strong defensive lines. Worst of all was the undetected September 5 arrival of the battered but still formidable II SS Panzer Korps at a rest area near the attack zone. Things were rapidly going to hell for Montgomery's plan.

The armored thrust slowed to a crawl. The British armored forces were simply too lacking in mechanized infantry to effectively clear German antitank resistance that hindered the advance. The Germans crushed the isolated British 1st Airborne Division and the Polish 1st Airborne Brigade at the crucial Arnhem bridge. The only lasting accomplishment was the capture of a deep, hard to hold salient into German territory. *Market Garden* was analyzed in excruciating detail, and prompted a unique apology of sorts from Montgomery. Allied airborne forces paid a terrible price because the British armored force was handed a nut it was never designed to crack.

# Hitler's Great Gamble—The Ardennes

Hitler was determined to throw the Western Allies back in hopes of a negotiated peace. Unternehmen *Wacht am Rhein* (Operation *Watch on the Rhine*) was an overly ambitious plan to drive through the densely forested Ardennes, recapture Antwerp, and cut off four Allied armies to the north. The plan depended heavily upon surprise and the capture of Allied stores, particularly fuel.

Through rigidly enforced secrecy and Allied overconfidence that Germany was too weak to attempt a major offensive, Hitler achieved his surprise. The Germans assembled a force of 400,000 men, 1,200 tanks, tank destroyers, and assault guns, and 4,200 artillery pieces. The entire plan hinged upon a rapid breakthrough in the Ardennes, opening the way for a mechanized dash to Brussels and Antwerp.

On December 16, the Germans broke through at a relatively quiet sector. The rupture was completely within the American operational zone, but in a bold move to simplify command structure, Eisenhower placed American troops on the northern flank under command of Montgomery. Stubborn resistance on the Elsenborn Ridge on the northern shoulder of the bulge and failure to capture the road junction at St. Vith diverted German forces southward. Stiffening American resistance fatally delayed the German onslaught and forced Kampfgruppe Peiper's *schwerpunkt* off course. The Germans failed to capture the fuel depot at Stavelot. Clogged roads thwarted German efforts to reinforce Peiper, and the attack lost momentum. Peiper was blocked at La Gleize; on December 23 the once-proud *panzer* troops were forced to break out on foot.

German forces were able to advance further in the south, but an epic resistance by American airborne troops at Bastogne slowed the breakthrough. Bastogne was a major highway nexus, and failure to capture it created major traffic jams. In the center the 2nd Panzer Division and Panzer Lehr fared better. Bypassing centers of resistance, the *panzers* came within sight of the Meuse River crossings. On December 23 the sun reappeared, and Allied fighter-bombers began the work of slaughtering the trapped German units. The exposed 2nd Panzer was cut off by the American 2nd Armored Division, and despite efforts by Panzer Lehr to relieve them they were forced to abandon their equipment.

On January 1, 1945, Eisenhower instructed Patton, on the south, and Montgomery, on the north, to pinch off the bulge. Patton had already charged in to relieve Bastogne, but the meticulous Montgomery balked at committing to an attack until January 3. By that date huge numbers of the enemy had escaped the trap.

Restricted spaces, rough terrain, and a tangled network of poor roads was not the terrain demanded by German doctrine. The German offensive was brought down by failure to accept the unsuitability of the terrain to large-scale armored operations with the types of vehicles that now predominated in the German army. Hitler was blinded by the 1940 success in which German columns of light tanks had advanced quickly through the weakly defended Ardennes. This time the attack was against prepared Allied positions under appalling weather conditions, and the

German armor was not nimble Panzer I and Panzer IIs, but lumbering, fuel-swilling Konigstigers (King Tigers) and Jagdtiger heavy tank destroyers. The Germans had erred badly, ignoring their own carefully crafted armored doctrine.

In the end the fighting delayed Allied plans for a thrust into Germany by five to six weeks. Germany had squandered its armored and manpower reserves on the Western Front. For the Western Allies the next 125 days would be primarily a bitter slog through Germany, an infantry fight with armored probes deep into German resistance.

## Clash of Titans—the Eastern Front

The struggle between the forces of Nazi Germany and the Soviet Union was gigantic in the number of tanks involved, but it was at its heart both a war of attrition and a struggle for territorial objectives. Both are the stuff of infantry combat, and the war was fought primarily by huge infantry forces.

By late 1940 Germany dominated all of Western Europe with the exception of Britain. Germany had never foreseen the need for amphibious warfare, and had neither the equipment nor the doctrine. Thwarted by the Royal Air Force and the English Channel, Hitler turned on his onetime ally, the Soviet Union.

The vast expanses of Russia were in one sense ideal for the *blitzkrieg* doctrine, in other ways a deadly trap. Vast open spaces allowed almost unlimited scope for maneuver, and allowed an attacker multiple routes to overwhelm a limited number of key objectives. But Germany was grossly unprepared for the logistical and transport nightmares presented by the deep battle space on the Russian scale. Spaces were huge, roads poor to non-existent, and the railway network limited.

In 1941 the Soviet Union possessed enormous resources of manpower and military equipment, and even many of their older tanks were superior to the tanks that formed the backbone of the Wehrmacht and SS armored forces. But in an inexplicable reversal in doctrine, in late 1939 the Soviets had disbanded the tank corps, dispersing tanks into infantry division control. A year later the Soviets reinstated the armored corps, but reconstruction was slow and confused. Stalinist purges eliminated so many senior officers that the Soviet forces were like a gigantic headless chicken. A notable exception was Zhukov, hero of Khalkin Ghol, who was elevated to Chief of the General Staff, where in January 1941 he helped conduct war games that centered on war with Germany.

Stalin resolutely ignored portents of a German invasion, relying upon his non-aggression pact with Hitler, and on June 22, 1941, Operation *Barbarossa*—though long-anticipated by many Soviet leaders—achieved strategic surprise. The onslaught along the entire German–Soviet border was an achievement never again repeated. The potentially decisive Soviet armored force was rendered useless by the chaos of the ongoing reconstitution: many units were without fuel, communications, spare parts, ammunition, or leadership. The stunning success of *Barbarossa* was due more to this Soviet disorganization than to any merits of German doctrine. Stalinist purges were accelerated in an effort to affix blame, and on July 29 Zhukov was demoted for advocating the evacuation of Kiev in order to trade space for time. By fall the Germans had pushed the Soviets to the gates of Moscow and stood poised to sever the main Soviet transport routes of fuel from the Caucasus. Then the German offensive ground to a stop, the victim of brutal winter and limited logistical capabilities.

The Soviets had bought breathing space, and now were prepared to counterattack and test their deep-battle doctrine, albeit on a small scale. The winter battles met with limited success, and in spring the Soviets transitioned back to a defensive posture. In mid-1942 Hitler shifted the strategic *schwerpunkt* southward, attacking the chokepoint of petroleum transport along the Volga River at Stalingrad. Again the German offensive faltered on logistical shortages, and Hitler's decision to pursue two goals, Stalingrad *and* the Caucasus oil fields. The Soviets pinched off the offensives and by early December the German Sixth Army was trapped and starving in Stalingrad.

In the summer of 1943 the Germans attempted to destroy the Soviet Kursk salient, but kept postponing the attack to await the arrival of more and newer tanks. The Soviets, aware of the plan, used the time to construct the deepest antitank defenses in history. When the Germans finally attacked, the fighting near Prochorovka saw the biggest tank battle in history with over a thousand tanks. When the German offensive bogged down in the deep defense, the Soviets transitioned into the deep-battle, attempting to cut off huge German forces by counterattacks north and south of the Kursk salient, and the two sides fought themselves to a standstill. German losses were enormous, and the battle spelled the end for their strategic offensives.

Germany was now fighting an industrial production battle it could not possibly win. Annual German fighting vehicle manufacturing increased five-fold between 1941 and 1944, but the Soviet Union had a head start. From 1941 through 1945 the Soviets built 99,500 tanks and self-propelled guns with another 7,000 tanks supplied by the United States and Britain. Germany produced 60,600, and was fighting a multi-front war.

From late 1943 the Soviets commenced an unrelenting series of offensive operations to push back the German armies in battles too numerous to describe. Many of these offensives dwarfed anything seen on the Western Front, but the climax was Operation *Bagration* (June 22–August 19, 1944). *Bagration* is less known than Kursk, but was a disastrous German defeat with the loss of all or major parts of three field armies spearheaded by tanks. The huge offensive was the first true test of the deep-battle doctrine on its intended scale, and began with three major breakthrough operations which encircled and destroyed several German corps. The most dispassionate (and lowest) estimate of German losses by Steve Zaloga is 300,000–375,000 men, and enormous numbers of vehicles. Germany could not possibly recover from such a loss, especially in the face of major losses in France.

The Soviets were never able to attain the single strategic victory not only because of Wehrmacht resilience, but primarily because

*With sloped armor and a 7.62cm main gun, high mobility on soft ground, and extreme mechanical reliability, the T-34/76 came as a terrible shock to the Germans in 1941. (Cansière)*

Soviet deep-battle doctrine inevitably foundered on logistics and lack of sufficient trucks. Although there was mechanized infantry, and the Soviets developed *tankovyy desant* (tank rider) tactics, the majority of infantry remained foot-borne, and much of the artillery relied upon horse traction. As a result *glubokaya bitva* (deep-battle) offensives inevitably ground to a stop as the Soviet armies outran their logistics. Their advance was reduced to stop and go motion as railway and horse-drawn transport stockpiled sufficient materials for the next great lunge. No matter, as the Germans were never again in a position to exploit a delay. From then until final victory the Soviets would rule in a war of attrition on a grand scale.

## Finis in Asia

Long before the German surrender the Allies commenced planning for an assault upon the Japanese home islands.

*The IS-3 and its derivative T-10 were the culmination of the Soviet heavy tank designs. With its small target profile, sloped armor, and powerful 122-mm main gun, it was a specialized tank-killer. (Gilbert)*

Operation *Olympic*, the invasion of Kyushu, projected the first significant use of American heavy tanks, the M26s. Most tanks would be the new M4A3 POA-CWS-H5, armed with both a 105-mm howitzer and a long-range flame gun, proven components of "blowtorch and corkscrew" tactics.

With Japan already staggering under the American onslaught, the Soviets declared war on August 8, 1945, after the atomic bombing of Hiroshima. The Soviets poured more than a million men into Manchuria and northeastern China, and 5,500 Soviet tanks and self-propelled guns overwhelmed the 1,500 obsolescent tanks of the Japanese Kwantung Army.

# CHAPTER 4

## THE COLD WAR AND WARS OF NATIONAL LIBERATION

*Carry the battle to them. Don't let them bring it to you. Put them on the defensive and don't ever apologize for anything.*

President Harry S. Truman

THE END OF WORLD WAR II did not mark the end of hostilities, only a realignment of adversaries. The Soviet Union's massive conventional army seemed poised to overrun Western Europe, spearheaded by overwhelming numbers of tanks. A decades-long faceoff between the North Atlantic Treaty Organization (NATO) countries and the Soviets and their Eastern European puppet states (the Warsaw Pact) would spread to other parts of the globe as proxy wars, and profoundly affect development of the tank as a weapons system.

The two sides chose dramatically different doctrinal approaches to a potential war in Europe, with tank designs reflecting those decisions. From its experiences against the Nazi armies in the recent war, Soviet strategists adhered to the doctrine commonly (though probably incorrectly) attributed to Joseph Stalin that "Quantity has a quality all its own." The Soviets would emphasize production of vast numbers of tanks that were good enough to get the job done: tanks and their crews were an expendable asset in the quest for battlefield dominance. Faced with the possibility of hordes of enemy tanks, the American and Western European nations started down a perhaps perilous path of emphasizing technical superiority over quantity, the dead-end path Nazi Germany had chosen.

In practice such an apparent dichotomy proved more than a bit simplistic. The difference was that the United States in particular could, if politics and economics permitted, have both quality and quantity. In turn Soviet designers, freed of the threat of Stalinist purges, proved quite innovative. Though overshadowed by the nuclear threat, a design race was on.

One result common to both sides was a two-decade-long evolution in tank doctrine. World War II had seen a tripartite division of tank types: light tanks for reconnaissance (American Stuarts and the German Luchs), medium tanks for general combat and infantry support (American M4s and Soviet T-34s), and heavy tanks for assaulting fixed defenses but more commonly as specialized tank killers (German Tigers and the Soviet IS-3s). The light tanks all but disappeared, eclipsed by aerial reconnaissance and other types of vehicles that could fulfill the role. The heavy tanks briefly morphed into specialized dinosaurian tank killers. Technological advances meant that the medium tank would eventually evolve into the concept of the all-purpose Main Battle Tank (MBT) combining the firepower of World War II super-heavy tanks, the armor protection of a heavy tank, and the light tank's mobility combined into the size and weight of a medium tank. For economic and logistical reasons, the MBT was the future.

This evolution was driven by two factors, perceived survivability and differing doctrines. The light tanks had little perceived survivability. Soviet doctrine was relentlessly offensive, and fundamentally dated to the "deep battle doctrine" of the 1930s. Slow, heavy tanks and assault guns would be employed as "breakthrough" vehicles, followed by a flood of MBTs to exploit the breakthrough. NATO, and Western doctrine in general, was more defensively oriented. The assumption was that an initial Soviet onslaught must first be blunted. To this end antitank weapons and MBTs would engage enemy tanks at relatively close ranges. Heavy tanks, with powerful long-range guns would be in overwatch positions to engage and destroy attacking Soviet heavy tanks, and support counterattacks with long-range fire.

## The French Complication

Following the 1949 creation of NATO, France's limited industrial capacity forced the continued use of American M4s and a few salvaged German Panther tanks. France launched a development program for the AMX-50, conceived as a medium tank, but the design evolved into a heavy tank. The 120-mm main gun was housed in a unique oscillating turret, which provided improved accuracy while the tank was in motion. The project was eventually aborted by high costs and the purchase of the new American M47 medium tank.

French military industry worked on a light tank project with a view toward replacing the old World War II tanks. The vehicle was to be rapidly deployable to the colonies and needed to be as light as possible (13 tons) for air transport. The new vehicle's purpose was reconnaissance and tank destroying. The tank's armor was to be reduced to a minimum and the oscillating turret was adopted because of its light weight. Interested by the concept, the United States funded the project and in 1948 the first AMX13 prototype was built. The engine was mounted in the front, and the armor could resist only heavy machine-gun fire.

The Americans were impressed by the fast tank (60km/h) with a powerful 75-mm gun. One crewmember was replaced by an automatic loader, two-drum magazine with six rounds each. This allowed a rapid rate of fire, but it had a disadvantage: it took nearly an hour to reload the two magazines. The AMX13

*The immediate post-World War II era witnessed considerable experimentation like the French AMX13 with its peculiar oscillating turret. The main gun was fixed and the upper part of the turret—and crew— tilted up and down to accomplish elevation of the main gun. (Cansière)*

was finally adopted by the French Army, despite its weight (15 tons), which was still light even for a tank destroyer.

The AMX13 was produced in many variants and exported to 30 countries. It was deployed overseas for the first time during the Algerian war, where it played a minor role.

The French initially participated in a program to design a universal NATO "European tank." In 1958 newly elected President Charles De Gaulle ended participation to "preserve French nuclear independence," and France began its own tank design program. The AMX30 had a conventional turret mounting a 105-mm main gun, but emphasized mobility, with reduced armor. The definitive prototype of the AMX30 was completed in 1966, the year De Gaulle finally withdrew from NATO to "free France from American domination."

By the 1970s the AMX30 was outclassed by new Soviet T-80s; again, France and West Germany tried and failed to work together on a replacement. The French knew they couldn't equal the number of tanks produced by the Eastern powers. Instead, they would produce an MBT incorporating the latest technologies.

A new tank entered limited service in 1986, named for Général Philippe Leclerc, who had liberated Paris in August 1944.

# The Heavy Tanks

The Soviets were the primary and most persistent advocates of the heavy tank. Several heavy tank designs had seen successful service in World War II, and development continued apace. The definitive model was the IS-3 with its long 122-mm gun, distinctive inverted-boat-like front hull and "dishpan" turret. Only about 350 were built by war's end, and it arrived only just in time for the victory parades in Germany. The improved IS-3M model featured better quality welding of the complex hull front, and introduced jettisonable external fuel tanks.

The IS-3 and IS-3M were long the backbone of the heavy tank regiments of Soviet field armies. Several new designs were tested, but the only one to enter service was the IS-10, basically an IS-3M with an extended chassis, thicker armor, improved engine, and a new cannon. It was redesignated the T-10 in the de-Stalinization of the 1950s.

Many IS-3/T-10 are displayed in various museums and as monuments, but few saw actual use outside of the Soviet Union. About a hundred IS-3Ms were exported to Egypt and saw service in the 1967 Six Day War. Perhaps the strangest odyssey was an IS-3 displayed on a concrete pedestal in the Ukraine as a war memorial. In 2014 pro-Russian separatists pulled it down and somehow got it running for brief use in the Novorossiya (New Russian) War. There is no record of whether or not the cannon was ever rendered operable, but it was recaptured by Ukrainian government forces and stuck back onto its plinth.

In May 1946, even the long-delayed American heavy tank of the World War II era, the M26, was reclassified as a medium tank. Stemming from changing doctrine, a brief Western flirtation with heavy tanks began. American and British designers had toyed with heavy tanks, but in World War II the difficulties of transporting heavy tanks across oceans and issues of diversion of manufacturing resources hamstrung the programs (with the exception of the Churchill infantry tank). In the Cold War era the British heavy tank program peaked with Conqueror, a 64-ton monster armed with the same 120-mm rifled cannon as its peer, the American M103. Production of the Conqueror Mark I began in 1955 with 20 vehicles, and 185 of the improved Mark II were built. The tank served only in West Germany from 1955 until 1966.

The first and only American heavy tank was the M103 series. At 65 tons, the initial vehicles were underpowered, a situation soon remedied by introduction of a more powerful diesel engine. The 120-mm cannon round was so heavy that the bulbous turret accommodated two loaders, one to load the projectile, the other the propellant casing.

Western tank doctrine was evolving, and the heavy tanks faced the more general tactical movement problem that very few European highway bridges could safely support their weight.

As the U.S. Army lost interest in the M103 project, the U.S. Marine Corps faced a different strategic problem. The Marines were to be a highly mobile force to "hold the line" against a Soviet offensive anywhere from Norway to Turkey, and would have to counter Soviet forces until the Army arrived. In a very unusual move the Marines took over final development of the M103, developed their own variant, the M103A2, and became its primary user. One company of the tank battalion assigned to each Marine Corps division would be equipped with the M103. One Army battalion in Germany (899th Tank Battalion, later redesignated 2nd Battalion, 33rd Armor) was temporarily equipped with M103A2s "loaned" from Marine stocks. The last M103A2s were withdrawn from Marine Corps service in 1974.

In NATO the British and the U.S. Army had somewhat different doctrines for the use of heavy tanks. The British integrated heavy tanks down to the troop (company) level, while

*The monstrous M103A2 was the only operational American heavy tank, used primarily by the U.S. Marine Corps. (U.S.M.C. via Ken Estes)*

the U.S. Army concentrated its few heavy tanks into the single battalion. In the middle were the U.S.M.C., which had tank battalions consisting of three medium tank companies supported by a fourth heavy tank company.

# Light Tanks

Like the heavy tank, the light tank was in eclipse, though the AMX-13 finally ended its long career in the 1990s. A new threat was emerging, and it was difficult to seal the oscillating turret against nuclear, bacteriological and chemical weapons.

The Americans were among the last to scrap the strategically mobile light tank concept, introducing the M551 Sheridan in 1969. Because of a new tank policy, the term light tank was no longer acceptable, and the vehicle was designated an "Armored Reconnaissance/Airborne Assault Vehicle."

Many countries experimented with peculiar hybrids to fill the light tank niche, usually cannon-armed turrets fitted to armored personnel carriers. The most heavily armed was the Australian M113 Fire Support Vehicle, an American M113 tracked personnel carrier fitted with the turret and 75-mm cannon from the British Saracen armored car. Other examples (among many) of this class were the tracked British Scimitar and Scorpion Armored Reconnaissance Vehicles, armed with 30-mm and 76-mm cannon respectively.

The traditional roles of the light tank were eventually usurped by a new class, the Infantry Fighting Vehicle (IFV), armed with light cannon, missiles capable of destroying MBTs, and carrying a small contingent of infantry dismounts. Both the Soviet Union and America produced specialized reconnaissance versions of these inexpensive and versatile vehicles, the BRM-1 and M3 Cavalry Fighting Vehicle respectively.

## The Main Battle Tank

The extinction of the heavy tank was brought about by the rise of

Designed to be a true airborne vehicle, the **Sheridan** was delivered by the "Low-Altitude Parachute Extraction System" (LAPES), in which the aircraft skimmed the ground in the landing zone and the vehicle on a special pallet was pulled out by a drogue parachute. The Sheridan was designed around the Shillaleagh 152-mm gun/missile system which could function either as a large cannon or fire an antitank missile. The system proved to be overly complex, and the Sheridan fired primarily shells. In addition, the light weight was achieved by an expanded-plastic material sandwiched between aluminum plates, and the vehicle had low combat survivability. The M551 series served in the Vietnam War, in Operation *Just Cause* (Panama), and was phased out after Operation *Desert Storm*.

a new doctrinal concept, the Main Battle Tank (MBT) "universal tank." Improvements in armor technology and firepower meant that these medium-weight tanks had increased survivability on the battlefield, high speed and mobility, and were perfectly capable of killing their heavy opponents.

The obsolescence of most British tanks led to a new breakthrough, an evolutionary successor to the Cromwell cruiser tank and the first true MBT. The British Centurion was a World War II design, though the first tank arrived on mainland Europe in May 1945. The tank featured heavy armor, a new suspension design, powerful engine, and the unusual feature of a two-speed reverse transmission. The main gun was the tested 17-pounder (76.2-mm), with another unusual feature—a 20-mm Polsten automatic cannon in a ball mount on the left side of the turret front face.

For the United States and the USSR, an economic limitation was the sheer numbers of tanks produced by 1945. The United States was the more reluctant to acquire new tanks, declaring all but the final M4A3(HVSS)76-mm model obsolete. The M26 Pershing series and its evolutionary successor, the M46, were reclassified as medium tanks. Continued developments in the series included the short-lived M47 series, and the more widely used M48 series medium tanks. The Soviets continued the evolutionary development of the T-44, succeeded by the T-54, T-55, and T-62 medium tanks.

The 1960s were another period of rapid technological and doctrinal evolution, and the redefinition as MBTs was more a matter of doctrine than technical design. For the U.S. the M60 series introduced in 1960 was the first designated MBT. It was superficially similar to the M48 series and in many features an evolutionary step from the M48A2. The primary weapon was a more powerful 105-mm main gun, and overall armor protection was upgraded to reflect the new threats from helicopters, top-attack munitions, and nuclear radiation. The new main gun was the source of considerable debate, but after testing the designers settled upon the M68 105-mm cannon derived from the older British 20-pounder.

*The M48 series were the last of the American medium tanks, and the definitive tank of the Vietnam War. This vehicle helping free a mired-down tank south of Danang is equipped with a dozer blade. (USMC-HD)*

The M60A1 and M60A3 were improved models, but the M60A2 "Starship" armed with the 152-mm Shillelagh gun-missile system was a failure due to the complexities of the weapon system. The M60A2s were quickly scrapped, and the chassis mostly converted to armored bridge-layers. Originally conceived as interim design, with the failure of the MBT-70 program (see below) the M60 series remained in American service through Operation *Desert Storm* in January 1991. It became one of the most produced series of MBTs, and it remains in service with several countries.

In the 1960s Germany and the United States initiated a program to develop the futuristic MBT-70/Panzerkampfwagen 70. The design incorporated a host of innovations. A "kneeling" suspension allowed the tank to reduce its target profile, level the turret on uneven ground, or raise the hull for high-speed travel on rough terrain. The entire three-man crew (commander, gunner, and driver) was located in the turret, the driver sitting in a counter-rotating turret so that he always faced forward, but the driver turret could in emergency be switched to a rear-facing position that allowed the tank to be driven backward at high speed.

*The Soviet T-55, like this example abandoned by the Iraqi Army, was typical of post-World War II Soviet designs, with a "frying pan" turret, infra-red spotlight, and external fuel drums barely visible on the rear. (Department of Defense)*

The main weapon was the Shillelagh gun-missile system, with an autoloader and laser range-finder, and introduced combustible-case ammunition in which the shell casing was part of the propellant charge. A remotely controlled 20-mm cannon was provided for use against aircraft and secondary targets. Crew protection was improved by two-layer spaced armor, anti-radiation crew-space lining, and air filtration against chemical and biological weapons.

The development of the MBT-70 was finally cancelled because of a host of problems. Drivers became disoriented by the motion of the counter-rotating turret, the main gun ammunition was both prone to moisture damage and cooking off (premature detonation of the propellant) from heat buildup in the main gun chamber, and the turbine engine was prone to damage by dust. By 1969 the development costs were spiraling out of control, and the project was cancelled in January 1970. An American successor, the XM803, proved equally complex and was cancelled in December 1971. The MBT-70 was a dead-end, though several design concepts were resurrected in the M1 development.

Other countries developed indigenous MBTs, including West Germany (Leopard, after failure of the MBT-70 program), France

(Leclerc), Britain (Challenger), China, Italy, Japan, India, Sweden, Switzerland, and Russia. Of these, the Leopard proved to be the most robust and popular design. The original Leopard 1 was used by eight primary users, and a large number have been passed on to six secondary users. In 2017, the next-generation Leopard 2 is in use by 17 countries, with four more planning or considering its adoption.

The British had since 1966 relied upon the Chieftain, at the time of its inception arguably the most advanced medium tank in the world. But the modern British MBT came from an unexpected direction. The fall of the Shah of Iran (1979) left the British without a market for an advanced tank designed for Iran, and the British Army adopted the tank in 1983. Challenger 1 was the first tank to use Chobham armor. The exact details of the armor remain classified, but it is a layered composite of ceramics, metal, and elastic layers that resist both HEAT and sabot rounds.

The advanced Challenger 2 was Britain's first true MBT, adopted in 1998. With advanced Dorchester armor, Challenger 2,

In 1967 Sweden accepted the unique **Stridsvagen 103**, or S-Tank, a vehicle that blurred boundaries since it was by design a tank-destroyer but by doctrine a tank. An analysis of World War II tank losses led to a doctrinal decision to eliminate the turret, the most commonly struck part of a tank. The target profile of the S-Tank was extremely low, and its fixed 105-mm rifled main gun was traversed by turning the entire vehicle, the elevation controlled by adjusting the suspension. Although the design received favorable reviews by British, American, and Norwegian analysts, it was a bit too specialized as a tank-killer. The concept never gained traction, and the last S-Tanks were removed from service in 1997.

*The French Leclerc is typical of the next generation of MBTs, with supplementary external armor, laser range-finder box on the right side of the turret, wind sensor on the turret roof, and an armored shield for the roof-mounted machine gun. (Cansière)*

alone among MBTs, still uses a rifled cannon. The tank has not been widely adopted, equipping only Britain and Oman's (38 tanks) armored forces.

By 1961 the Soviets had added a new wrinkle in their tank doctrine, with the adoption of the T-62 medium tank. The design introduced new features like an auto-ejection system for spent shell casings, but the new tank was expensive to manufacture, and carried a high maintenance burden. The solution was the introduction of a two-tier doctrine in which certain units would be equipped with the T-62 "premium" tank, while most were equipped with a "standard" tank like the less expensive T-55. The theory was that the premium tank units would be utilized at more critical points, and as breakthrough units.

The great success story of the Cold War era was the T-72 series, with over 20,000 built and used by 40 countries. With such a variety of users, and prolonged production history (1973 to the present) the T-72 has been produced in a bewildering array of models: five basic models and at least six specialized variants by the Soviets/Russians alone, and seven licensed foreign models.

In addition to the usual low profile, simplicity, and low cost, some specific design criteria to fit Soviet doctrine included comprehensive nuclear/biological/chemical protection, and lighter weight for frail Eastern European bridges, and it is ideally suited to the Soviet deep-battle doctrine.

Some models of the T-72 incorporated ceramic rods in the vulnerable turret front armor, and the bulging turret faces gave rise to the nickname "Dolly Parton" (T-72A), and later "Super Dolly Parton" (T-72B) models with composite ceramic plates inside the turret front. The T-72 retained a shell ejection system like that of the T-62, but a carousel-type automatic loader with rounds stored beneath the turret floor replaced the human loader. An unfortunate characteristic of the autoloader is that in the tight confines of the turret it tends to catch the gunner's arm and shove it into the breech if a special protective plate is not installed.

Given the location of army bases and production facilities, in the dissolution of the Soviet Union many T-72s fell into the hands of the breakaway states, and the tank is still produced in old Soviet states and former Warsaw Pact nations. The T-72 also holds the distinction of seeing probably the most extensive combat use of any MBT, with involvement in at least 29 conflicts at various scales.

After firing, the **T-62**'s turret rotated to the vehicle center line, the spent casing was ejected out the rear of the turret, the loader seated a new round, and in theory the gun returned to its previous point of aim. In practice it did not allow the gunner to quickly adjust his point of aim by observing impact of the previous round, slowed the rate of fire, and the hot shell casing sometimes missed the exit port and bounced around the turret interior.

# The Fall of China

The Chinese civil war temporarily subsided as both sides fought Japan, but then resumed with a vengeance. Chinese Nationalist KMT forces had American-supplied tanks from World War II including M4A4s, and various types of light tanks. The retreating Japanese had turned most of their more advanced Type 97 Chi-Has over to the KMT, but two were captured by the Communists. Mutinous Japanese sabotaged one, so the Chinese People's Liberation Army (PLA) was equipped with a grand total of one tank, though the PLA tank force grew as more Type 97s and American-made tanks were captured.

For years America continued to supply the KMT, but blundering and corruption caused a loss of faith and eventually America ceased to pour war material into the KMT, only to see it reappear in the hands of the PLA. A series of significant but little-known major battles resulted in huge losses of American-supplied materiel, and eventual retreat of the KMT onto Taiwan and smaller islands, where it continued to hold out. After the fall of China, the Soviet Union supplied some 1,800 T-34/85s, and the Chinese manufactured a copy, the Type 58.

# Korea

For all the fears of the Western nations, the first great clash with Communist forces came not in Europe but in remote Korea. It was not any local aspect of the feared global Communist assault on the democracies, but simply the inability of the Soviet Union and Communist China to control Kim Il Sung, the maniacal leader of North Korea. Korea had been partitioned into North and South at the end of World War II, and Kim was determined to reunite the county by force if necessary. Kim was encouraged by the U.S. decision not to provide South Korea with heavy weapons: other than 105-mm howitzers, the heaviest weapons in the South's arsenal were a few antiquated 57-mm and 37-mm antitank guns, and 27 old M8 armored cars with 37-mm guns.

In contrast, the North was lavishly equipped with Soviet weaponry, including T-34/85 tanks and SU-76 self-propelled artillery. The North had no real doctrine except vicious and unrelenting attacks. When the North attacked on June 25, 1950, many South Korean units fought brave but futile actions as the South's forces crumbled under the onslaught spearheaded by tanks. The Soviets were boycotting the United Nations and could not exercise their veto, and the United States was able to achieve UN approval to intervene.

American forces had grown soft on occupation duty in Japan. Another issue was that America, ever fearful of a Soviet attack in Europe, would not send its better-equipped and trained units. The war in Korea would be fought with World War II weapons. Worse, the heaviest American weapons immediately available were 105-mm howitzers and a few M24 Chaffee light tanks of the U.S. 78th Tank Battalion; the bridges in Japan could support nothing heavier. The M24s proved ineffective against the bigger T-34s, and usually just retreated in the face of enemy tanks.

Many of the final production version of the venerable Sherman, the M4A3(76mm)HVSS, were in depot storage in Japan. Reactivated and thrown piecemeal into battle, they proved equally ineffective. A handful of more modern U.S. Army M26 "depot queens" with their bigger 90-mm guns were also thrown into battle but were quickly lost to mechanical failures. Losses were commonly attributed to fan belt problems, but many failures may have been simple driver inexperience or poor maintenance.

Within weeks the North had pushed South Korean and American forces into a small perimeter around the port of Pusan, but reinforcements had begun to flow in even as Northern forces were becoming over-extended by their successes. American reinforcements included a brigade of Marines, with a company of M26 tanks in the hands of more experienced users.

The first armored clash came in the first battle of the Naktong on August 17, 1950. A dangerous gap in the American lines had developed, and a platoon of North Korean tanks and supporting infantry were rushing down a road toward the American rear areas. A platoon of Marine Corps M26s was hastily thrown into the gap. As the tanks advanced, an Army officer flagged down Sergeant Cecil Fullerton's tank leading the column and told him "Don't go up there! There's tanks up there!" "What do you think this thing is?" Fullerton shot back. "Get out of the way!"

The tank platoon under Lieutenant Granville G. Sweet, a former enlisted tank NCO in World War II, took up positions in a road cut. The North Koreans rushed confidently—and blindly—into an ambush. Fullerton's tank opened fire with tungsten-cored armor-piercing ammunition at close range, pumping a couple of rounds into a hapless T-34 to no apparent effect; there were none of the expected explosions. "You missed, Ski" Fullerton yelled at his gunner, Sergeant Stanley "Ski" Tarnowksi. "I don't miss, Sergeant Fullerton" Tarnowski replied. In fact, "It [the armor piercing round] just punched its way through armor. It went through the bow [machine gun], through the turret [base]... tore half the engine of that T-34 out, went on through, and hit on that hill over there, on Obong-ni Ridge." The infantry on the ridge radioed that they were taking friendly fire, so the tankers switched to high explosive, annihilating the North Korean tanks.

As more reinforcements poured in, the Marine Corps' First Tank Battalion spearheaded the Inchon landings, as their Army counterparts broke out of the Pusan perimeter and drove north. The fleeing North Koreans abandoned much of their armor as American and South Korean forces pushed toward the Chinese border at the Yalu River.

The surprise Chinese entry into the war in November 1950 pitted UN forces against a less understood and more unconventional foe. To maintain the element of surprise, avoid overwhelming UN airpower, and simply from tradition, the Chinese Communists attacked with a force that was exclusively infantry and man-portable weapons. In a few actions the Chinese were supported by a few surviving T-34/85 tanks, easily dealt with. In late November, massive "human wave" attacks overwhelmed many unprepared UN units and sent the U.S. Army west of the rugged mountainous spine of the Korean peninsula reeling into the longest retreat of its history. Yet even in totally unprecedented tactical conditions and facing bitter cold, the tanks played a role in the successful escape of units surrounded by Communist forces in eastern Korea. A single M26 spearheaded the epic attack that opened the crucial Toktong Pass to allow units to escape from the Chosin Reservoir.

The combat debut of the Centurion tank came during the long retreat. The 8th King's Royal Irish Hussars (KRIH) arrived just in time to join the UN retreat. At the Han River crossings north of Seoul a Centurion Mark III on the south shore came under fire from a Cromwell VII tank captured from the KRIH's own Reconnaissance Troop. The Centurion, *Caughao*, and another tank from Headquarters Troop, C Squadron returned fire, destroying the captured tank at a range of some 3,000 yards/2,740 meters. It was a phenomenal shot, justifying the new 20-pounder/84-mm gun. The British contingent deployed the last of the cruiser tanks, the Cromwell as reconnaissance vehicles, Centaurs as dozer tanks.

Even as the Communist offensive petered out from casualties and overextended logistics, UN resistance stiffened. In one of the final Chinese and North Korean efforts, on February 13, 1951, the U.S. Army's 23rd Regimental Combat Team reinforced with a company of tanks—under orders not to retreat—was surrounded by three Chinese divisions at Chipyong-ni. A relief column of a company of M46 tanks, three platoons of old M4A3s, and supporting units set out to relieve the surrounded regiment. Temporarily blocked by a wrecked bridge, and subjected to constant ambushes, on February 15 the column commander pared down his force to the tanks and a company of infantry to ride the tanks and protect against close assault by enemy infantry. Task Force Crombez laboriously fought its way past attackers armed with satchel charges and captured bazookas, with the loss of one M46, but at heavy cost to the infantry.

Sensing the enemy's weakening, the new American commander, Matthew Ridgway, ordered offensives *Killer* and *Ripper*. American intelligence mistakenly informed the tank crews that the Chinese were very superstitious and fearful of tigers and dragons, which led to some of the strangest markings ever applied to tanks. Whatever effect it might have had on the Chinese, it was a badly needed morale boost to the Americans who indeed "ripped" into the enemy with a vengeance. By early April UN forces had recaptured Seoul and pushed the enemy back to an irregular front roughly along the old border before heavy rains and the spring thaw bogged the offensive in deep mud.

Additional UN contingents were committed, mostly using American-supplied equipment to simplify logistics. Throughout the remainder of the conflict, UN armor dominated the battlefield. It is impossible to determine anything about Chinese tank doctrine—if indeed there was one—since Communist accounts were shrouded in ham-fisted propaganda. The Chinese reported their T-34/85 destroyed numerous American tanks, though more transparent American records state that Chinese armor was seldom if ever encountered in ground combat. (The report *Tank v Tank Combat in Korea* listed 119 "definite to possible" encounters, but this included air attacks by American planes and suspected sightings.)

As both sides settled into trench warfare, the M26 and later M46 tanks (an improved M26) were used by the U.S. Army and Marine Corps in different roles. The Marines used tanks more aggressively to support infantry raids, and tanks with dozer blades were used for front-line construction. The Army tended to use tanks more as fixed positions and heavy firepower to augment infantry weapons. Tanks were effectively used for precision fire at specific targets ("bunker busting"), since their flat trajectory fire was more precise and damaging than plunging artillery fire or aerial bombing. The most onerous duty reported by American tank crews was as long-range artillery. Many Communist guns outranged American artillery, so the tank guns were utilized by constructing dirt ramps to allow for indirect fire at high elevations. The tanks' turret traversing ring-gear was never designed for such angles, resulting in increased damage and failure. Tanks became propaganda pawns, as the Communists gleefully reported the destruction of tanks, real or imagined.

## The Vietnamese War

The proxy struggle in South Vietnam was the longest sustained war in recent history. North Vietnamese armored doctrine is virtually impossible to discern. South Vietnamese and U.S. Army and Australian armor doctrine would evolve as the tank again reverted to its primary role as an infantry support weapon.

Following the Japanese collapse in 1945 the French reoccupied Vietnam, under the leadership of Philippe Leclerc. Leclerc engineered a short-lived alliance with Communist leader Ho Chi Minh since Ho feared the Chinese far more than the French. When the Viet Minh were recognized by other Communist governments, the agreement broke down and the French reintroduced armor into Indochina in order to help suppress Communist nationalists.

The force included American M5A1s as well as captured Japanese tanks, reinforced in 1947–48 by old Hotchkiss H-39 light tanks. Beginning in 1950 the Americans began to supply military equipment, and LVT(A)-4s, though not technically tanks, proved particularly useful as mobile artillery in the marshy Mekong and Red River Delta regions.

Fearful of direct Chinese Communist involvement in the growing struggle, a few M4 tanks and M36 tank destroyers were sent to Vietnam, but served only as infantry support weapons. The French sought to compensate for their relative weakness by the use of mechanized *Groupements Mobiles* patterned after the

American regimental combat teams, and *Groupes d'Escadrones de Reconaissance* that generally included a small tank detachment. But the French were simply spread too thin.

Eventually the French launched an ambitious plan to establish an airhead at remote Dien Bien Phu, and lure Communist forces into a an area where the French thought the Communists would be stretched thin logistically. It was a fatal miscalculation. A major element of the force was ten M24 Chaffee light tanks, the Escadron de Marche du 1er Régiment de Chasseurs à Cheval, under Captain Yves Hervouet. The tanks were disassembled, flown into the airhead, and reassembled. The avowed purpose of the base was to conduct far-ranging patrols, in which the M24s participated.

On March 13, 1954, the Viet Minh began a massive artillery bombardment using American guns captured in China and Korea. The light tanks did heroic service in counterattacks and evacuating wounded from isolated positions. In the end Dien Bien Phu fell.

Although Dien Bien Phu was the iconic battle of the war, the final blow was the ambush and near total destruction of Groupement Mobile No. 100. The French high command ordered the evacuation of the Central Highlands. The road-bound column linked up with Groupement Mobile No. 42 and airborne troops, but the force suffered extraordinary casualties, and the loss of almost all heavy equipment. The eventual result was an armistice and partition of Vietnam, and when the French eventually departed, they turned over a motley assortment of about 450 tanks and tank destroyers to the new Army of the Republic of Vietnam.

By 1965 the Army of the Republic of Vietnam (ARVN) was equipped more or less exclusively by America, with over 200 M41 "Walker Bulldog" light tanks, and M113A1 armored personnel carriers in large numbers.

When the United States decided to actively engage in the Vietnamese fighting in 1965, American aircraft were first based at Danang near the demilitarized zone. After Viet Cong guerrillas destroyed several aircraft on the ground, America retaliated by bombing North Vietnam. Fearful of North Vietnamese air attacks, the United States installed Hawk missile batteries around Danang. On March 8, 1965, Marine infantrymen arrived to protect the missile batteries from ground attack. No one in President Lyndon Johnson's administration remembered that Marine Battalion Landing Teams were routinely supported by a platoon of tanks, so five M48A3 tanks clanked ashore. The uproar was immediate and loud. No matter that infantry, missile batteries, and fighter-bombers were scattered all about Danang. The five tanks were symbolic of a major "escalation" of the war.

As the buildup of American forces continued, Army and Marine Corps armored units continued to arrive. The tanks were just too useful as infantry support vehicles. Eventually two Marine Corps tank battalions and parts of a third were committed in Vietnam. The Army fielded three independent tank battalions attached to infantry divisions.

The Army tank units had the hardest initial experiences. Trained for European-style warfare, the tanks were first committed to futile mechanized sweeps across the countryside. The Viet Cong simply went to ground and let mines do their work. Army officers were quickly forced to revise doctrine to reflect the local situation, parceling out small tank detachments for infantry support.

The Vietnam War saw the last gasp of the light tank as a significant weapon. One of the less successful light vehicles was the M551 Sheridan. It was vulnerable to both rocket-propelled grenades (RPGs) and mines, as the propellant of the combustible-case ammunition often exploded when any weapon penetrated the hull, with catastrophic results.

The only ally to deploy armor to South Vietnam was Australia, who initially balked at sending tanks before deploying a troop of 20 Centurions in February 1968 as a test. The tanks quickly proved their value, and soon the infantry was reluctant to operate without them. By September three squadrons were operating in South Vietnam. Oddly the M113 Fire Support Vehicles (FSV) were not sent "in country" until mid-1971. By that time the Australians had learned the Viet Cong predilection for mines and RPGs, and the light tank surrogates were little used. The most intense tank combat came with the January 1968 Tet Offensive, when VC and NVA forces seized control of several South Vietnamese cities. The most brutal fighting was the recapture of Hue, the old Imperial Vietnamese capital. Seven Communist battalions took control of the city, with four more in the nearby countryside. They would be pitted against Task Force X-Ray, a cobbled together command of five American battalions and ten South Vietnamese battalions supported by a handful of Marine Corps tanks. The street fighting was incredibly brutal, as dozens of RPG rounds struck the tanks supporting infantry in the narrow streets.

Early in the fight Carl "Flash" Fleischmann was the driver of a headquarters tank from Third Tank Battalion fighting on the banks of the Perfume River when he saw a VC step into the open and fire an RPG at the tank. The rocket impacted the turret. "When that happened, Robert Hall, the tank commander, took the full brunt of the RPG" and another crewman was wounded. Fleischmann rode along with Hall to the aid station. "The doctor and the [medical] corpsman said there was nothing they could do for him because he had no face. Robert was holding onto me. They said 'Just hold onto him until he passes on'. He did." Typical of the fighting in Hue, Fleischmann walked back to the tank, grabbed a couple of replacements, and headed out again.

Throughout the month-long battle the tanks were everywhere: shelling the heavy masonry buildings, carrying loads of wounded, smashing through buildings to make safe passageways that avoided the fire-swept streets. The M48 tanks proved incredibly hard to destroy, but not so their human crews: some tanks went through as many as seven crews as replacements were airlifted into the city.

What no one realized at the time was that the Hue fighting would help shape future urban combat doctrine. Tanks and infantry cordoned off the city, preventing enemy escape, reinforcement, and resupply. These aspects would later emerge as part of the "battlespace shaping" doctrine for urban combat.

North Vietnamese armor saw limited use until the final days

of the war. Their first armored unit, the 202nd Regiment, was formed in 1959 and equipped with 35 T-34/85s and 16 CAY-76 (Soviet SU-76) self-propelled guns. By the early 1960s the NVA was attempting to modernize, and a second armored regiment, with T-34 and T-54 tanks, was formed in May 1965. The strength of the 202nd Regiment was augmented by T-54 medium tanks and PT-76 amphibious tanks. Later arrivals included Soviet T-55 tanks, Chinese Type 59 (T-54 copy) medium tanks and Type 62 light tanks, and Chinese Type 63 derivatives of the PT-76. For most of the war the North Vietnamese chose not to employ armor in the south, likely because of the formidable problems of moving heavy vehicles down the jungle tracks known as the Ho Chi Minh Trail, and vulnerability to American air attack.

The only tanks used against American forces were the PT-76s. On the night of February 6–7, 1968, tanks from the North Vietnamese 198 Tank Battalion supported the 24 Regiment in an attack on the American Special Forces base at Lang Vei.

The Americans spotted the tanks advancing toward the south side of the camp under the cover of heavy artillery fire, and three PT-76 tanks were ripped apart by 106-mm recoilless guns. On the north side three PT-76s broke into the camp and began to destroy bunkers with point-blank cannon fire. Tank-killer teams attacked the tanks with M72 hand-held antitank rockets (LAAWs) but the thinly armored tanks simply shrugged off the rockets—most likely an accident of the PT-76's design allowed them to survive. The small shaped-charge warheads could not penetrate very far inside a tank, and in the PT-76 there was a lot of open space to dissipate the explosive jet. The main ammunition storage in the PT-76 was in a metal box underneath the main gun near the center line of the vehicle. In short, you could punch a lot of holes in a PT-76 without hitting anything vital. It was a repeat of the experiences with the first American bazookas in North Africa during early 1943. The NVA eventually broke off the attack, but losses were heavy on both sides, including several tanks wrecked or abandoned.

In April 1969 the Special Forces camp at Ben Het came under

a series of attacks by North Vietnamese forces. A company of M48A3 tanks, supported by a pair of M42 "Duster" self-propelled 40-mm antiaircraft guns, was assigned to the defense of Ben Het and security of the road leading to it. Usually a platoon was based at Ben Het, the rest of the company at nearby Dak To.

Ben Het suffered under a constant rain of artillery fire from across the border in Cambodia. As in Korea, the tanks' longer-ranged 90-mm guns were used as indirect fire weapons, but even concrete-penetrating fuses failed to silence the enemy guns. In early March, company commander Captain John Stovall had come to the base since the local platoon leader had been wounded. On March 1 the enemy artillery went silent. At 2200 hours on March 2, Platoon Sergeant Hugh Havermale reported the sound of vehicle engines, and on March 3 South Vietnamese Civilian Irregular Defense Group (CIDG) reconnaissance patrols found indications that an attack was imminent.

At 2100 hours on March 3, the base began to receive heavy artillery fire. At about 2200 hours the Americans heard the rumble of heavy engines and the distinctive squeal of tracks, but could not see anything. The first NVA tank detonated a mine, setting fire to external stores on the tank. The firelight revealed three PT-76 tanks and a BTR-50 tracked personnel carrier. Then Stovall received a radio message that a CIDG patrol outside the defensive wire had spotted 8–15 more tracked vehicles approaching, and a fourth PT-76 very near the camp. Enemy flares burst overhead, revealing the positions of the American tanks.

Stovall jumped onto the engine deck of a tank just as a round from one of the enemy tanks struck, blowing him back onto the ground, heaving the wounded tank commander over the engine deck, and killing the loader and the driver. Other men from the company removed the casualties and put the tank back into action.

By this time a relief column was arriving from Dak To. With the loss of two tanks and a personnel carrier, the NVA began to withdraw. It was later determined that the tanks were from the NVA 4th Battalion, 202nd Armored Regiment, but it remains a mystery why no infantry from the NVA 66th Regiment supported the attack.

American forces prevailed in every battle of 1968 and 1969, but there was a collective loss of the political will to fight. As the Americans withdrawal began, the NVA began to move conventional forces some 1200 km south along the improved Ho Chi Minh Trail, including the 171st Tank Battalion.

In an attempt to limit NVA movement along the Ho Chi Minh Trail, the ARVN launched a major operation into the Plain of Jars border region of Laos and Cambodia. The rising dominance of the NVA was reflected in the increased role of the 26th Armored Regiment in driving out the ARVN and Thai forces.

The United States was transitioning to the new M60 MBT, so in the withdrawal of American forces in 1972, some 190 M48A3 tanks were turned over to the South Vietnamese. As the Soviets and Chinese jockeyed for positions of influence in Vietnam, the ascendant NVA received huge influxes of modern equipment, including 600 tanks.

As the U.S. withdrew, the NVA launched its Easter Offensive, aimed at strengthening its bargaining position in truce talks. Hundreds of

In addition to the major defining conflicts, the Soviet Union sponsored **"wars of national liberation"** anywhere the opportunity presented itself. The West, primarily America, countered by propping up right-wing regimes, all too often dictatorial, in sub-Saharan Africa, Latin America, and Asia. The result was a proliferation of tanks, often more as symbols of prestige rather than practical weapons. Armored units were sometimes referred to as "coup troops" for their intimidating involvement in regime changes of all political stripes. In general the Soviets supplied tanks from T-34 to T-55 models, the American tanks as old as the M4 series to modern M47s.

tanks spearheaded a major attacks, striking across the DMZ and from Laos and Cambodia to the west. The South Vietnamese had never faced a conventional armored force, and were quickly swept aside. With the aid of American air and naval gunfire assets (including an entire NVA tank battalion destroyed in a massive strike by B-52 bombers) the South Vietnamese fought the NVA to a standstill. The NVA gained a major foothold in the south, and made a key political point, but at heavy cost in manpower and weaponry. Losses included an estimated 134 T-54/T-55, 56 PT-76, and 60 T-34 tanks.

Undeterred, in October 1973 the NVA began massing corps-scale forces for another conventional onslaught. The Second Corps, included the renamed 203rd Tank Brigade, the Central Highlands Front included the 273rd Tank Regiment. Only the Fourth Corps Mekong Group had no armor contingent.

In December 1974 the NVA began a new series of conventional offensives, often spearheaded by tanks. The ARVN more or less matched the Communists in manpower and outnumbered them six to one in armored vehicles as the result of heavy NVA losses in 1972 not replaced by the Soviets and Chinese, age and deterioration of equipment, plus the NVA suffered from severe ammunition shortages. But the ARVN suffered from disastrously poor morale and was led by generals chosen for their political connections.

The offensive simply overwhelmed the better equipped but demoralized ARVN. In the Hue region the 4th Tank Company, 203rd Tank Brigade spearheaded attacks on ARVN positions, happily using captured M48 tanks.

By April 1975 the NVA had fought their way to the outskirts of Saigon, and the war was obviously lost. According to the official NVA history, at 1045 hours on April 30, NVA Type 59 tank number 843, commanded by Lieutenant Bui Quang, smashed its way through the steel gates of the Presidential Palace, the symbolic ending of the decades-long war. A quick-thinking crewman, Nguyễn Văn Thiệu, grabbed a flag and rushed up the stairs, becoming the first to raise the flag of the Provisional Revolutionary Government over the palace.

For the Vietnamese the war did not end. Their armored forces, now including captured M41 and M48 tanks, saw action in repulsing a Cambodian Khmer Rouge invasion and then invading Cambodia in 1978–79.

# China Resurgent

The new Chinese Communist regime initiated its own tank-building program with the Type 58, a copy of the T-34/85, and later the Soviets helped build a facility for manufacturing the Type 59 (Soviet T-54A). China faced its own unique problems with the terrain of southern China, where numerous waterways, frail bridges, and rice agriculture limited tank mobility. This led to an unusual rejuvenation of the light tank concept, with the Type 62 series.

Chinese–Soviet relations chilled as the two vied for influence during the Vietnam War, culminating in the brief armed clash in 1979. China then expanded its tank-construction program using some features of a captured Soviet T-62 as the basis for its Type 69, and the derivative Type 79. The PLA found the Type 69 marginally acceptable, but the low cost, simple operation, and ease of maintenance made it popular with buyers like Iran and Iraq.

The introduction of the Type 80 in 1981 triggered a power struggle within the Chinese military, with familiar factions. One group advocated a Soviet T-72 type with a small crew and low survivability, the other a design that resembled the new Israeli Merkava. Perhaps predictably, the first faction won out.

A warming of relationships with the West permitted an influx of new technology, and the growth of the Chinese tank industry (greatly simplified here) is illustrative of the often convoluted internationalization of late 20th-century arms industries. The new second-generation Type 88 MBT kept the same basic hull and turret as the Type 79, but with a German diesel engine, Austrian 105-mm main gun, British laser range-finder and fire-control system, and a new Chinese-designed suspension.

The next generation, the Type 90 (Type 90-I for the export market) incorporated modular armor, a British engine (from the Challenger 2 MBT) and French transmission (from the Leclerc). When the Pakistani nuclear tests resulted in a Western arms embargo the primary Chinese player in the export market, NORINCO, exhibited the Type 90-IIM at the 2001 Abu Dhabi Defense Expo (by this time weapons had become an international trade commodity) and it was adopted. When the Chinese engine proved unreliable, China incorporated a Ukrainian diesel engine to produce the Type 90–IIM. This model was adopted by Pakistan, and it served as the basis for the domestically produced al-Khalid MBT.

## The Americans

In the post-Vietnam era the United States turned its attentions back to a possible war in Europe, and concluded that qualitative superior was the only possible counter to numerically superior Soviet forces. As the primary guarantor of NATO, the United States was severely impacted by failure of the MBT-70 program.

At this point in time a new tank requirement became part of a dispute over strategic doctrine. The new tank was to be but one component of a new force. In a 1961 speech President Dwight Eisenhower had warned of the dangers of too close a tie between the military and industry:

> This conjunction of an immense military establishment and a large arms industry is new in the American experience. The total influence—economic, political, even spiritual—is felt in every city, every State house, every office of the Federal government. We recognize the imperative need for this development. Yet we must not fail to comprehend its grave implications….
>
> In the councils of government, we must guard against the acquisition of unwarranted influence, whether sought or unsought, by the military-industrial complex. The potential for the disastrous rise of misplaced power exists and will persist.

As floods of money poured into weapons procurement programs, procurement officers sought to advance their careers by championing failing projects. In a 1988 graduate school thesis by Army Captain Dale E. Wilson, he recounted the frustrations of Elgin Braine's 1918 mission, and compared it to

> recent attempts by procurement personnel working in concert with civilian manufacturers to conceal real or alleged design flaws in such systems as the Bradley Infantry/Cavalry Fighting Vehicle, the Sgt York Division Air Defense Gun [twin radar-controlled guns on an MBT chassis, cancelled in 1985] ....
>
> The question we must ask ourselves today, given the layered bureaucracies with overlapping lines of authority or special interests that exist in the Department of Defense and individual service weapons procurement agencies, is: Are we better off than we were in 1918?

Such a question seemed particularly relevant when the expensive XM803 program produced a simplified and less expensive tank, but with capabilities no better than the M60 it was intended to replace. The project was cancelled in 1971.

Building on the MBT-70 program, the M1 Abrams series was introduced in 1980, but retained a 105-mm main gun. The armor design was a fundamental departure from the cast steel that had characterized American design for fifty years. The variant of Chobham composite armor could only be manufactured as flat plates, leading to an angular hull and turret. In 1986 the M1A1 with a 120-mm smoothbore gun and improved imaging and fire control systems, improved armor, and improved nuclear/biological/chemical protection, entered service. Most crucial was the gun/targeting system that gave the Abrams the capability to outrange Soviet-made T-62s and T-72s.

In 1988 improved armor incorporating a depleted uranium mesh was introduced as the M2A2HA, or Heavy Armor variant. Continuing improvements in armor and fire control resulted in the M1A2 SEP (Systems Enhancement Package). Combat experience resulted in ongoing improvements such as improved

*The M1 series tank still dominates the battlefield. This example in Iraq has a TUSK-upgraded protection package as indicated by the external machine-gun mount above the loader's hatch. (Department of Defense)*

communications, addition of the CROWS remote-control external machine gun, and various generations of the Tank Urban Survival Kit (TUSK). TUSK was introduced in 2006 as the result of urban warfare experience in Iraq, and included External Reactive Armor (ERA) kits to cover the side skirts, slat armor to protect the vulnerable rear, defensive fragmentation grenade dischargers, improved shielding for the vehicle commander when exposed for better situational awareness, and a spotlight for the external machine gun.

A significant problem was the increasing weight, so the M1A3 under development includes weight-reduction features like a lighter main gun, lighter suspension, fiber-optic wiring, and a new engine that reduces weight by two tons. In all, the M1 series was destined to become a very successful design, equipping six nations in addition to the United States.

# The Waning Days of the Cold War

The most marked indication of the Soviet decline was the ill-advised invasion of Afghanistan. After the fall of a Soviet-backed government, the new regime grew increasingly hostile to Soviet influence. On December 24, 1979 the Soviets invaded Afghanistan, spearheaded by armor of the Soviet 40th Army's two Motor Rifle Divisions. By mid-1980 anti-Soviet insurgents were receiving massive support from America and Saudi Arabia through Pakistan. The highly mechanized Soviet force, consisting largely of conscripts, was structurally and doctrinally trained for operations against similar European armies, utilizing the deep-battle doctrine. The Afghans would not cooperate. Observers repeatedly noted the reluctance of mechanized infantry to disembark from the perceived safety of their personnel carriers. Tanks were mostly older models like the T-55 and T-62.

The developing Soviet strategy was to have most of the fighting done by Afghan infantry, with Soviet troops—including armor—in a supporting role. The strategy failed miserably, and soon the Soviets were penned into the cities; insurgents controlled some 80 percent of the countryside. The Soviets then switched to a strategy of repression, launching armored forays supported by helicopters to destroy villages and terrify or kill the occupants.

The Afghan resistance was fragmented and disorganized, but nevertheless efficient in debilitating the Soviets. In rugged desert and mountain terrain that favored infantry operations, the heavily mechanized Soviet forces were less successful than light infantry and covert political operatives. One innovation was the *bronegruppa* (armored group), "a temporary grouping of four–five tanks, BMPs or BTRs—or any combination." The armored personnel carriers "deployed without their normally assigned infantry squad on board and fight away from their dismounted troops. The grouping has a significant direct-fire capability and serves as a maneuver reserve."

Liberally supplied with mines and RPGs, the insurgents staged ambushes of the often road-bound armored units.

Armored forces proved not only ineffective in this kind of war, but often counterproductive as images of burned-out vehicles and incinerated crewmen provided lucrative propaganda for the insurgents. Soviet forces tried to conceal losses for morale and political reasons. One general covertly watched an armored column returning from an ambush: "Disabled tanks and trucks were towed, carefully camouflaged, inside the column."

Ground down by the insurgency, between May 1988 and February 1989 the Soviets ignominiously withdrew from the country.

For its part the United States deployed tanks in a number of small-scale interventions. Operation *Just Cause*, the intervention in Panama saw the only "combat" airdrop of M551 Sheridans when ten were airdropped (two were wrecked in the process), and another four were delivered by conventional means. Somewhat more successful was the deployment of a platoon of M60A1s to Grenada, October 25–26, 1993. In a logistical snafu the tanks were put ashore without main gun ammunition, but fortunately Grenadan troops fled at the squealing sound of the tank tracks.

## The Post-Soviet Era—Chechnya

In the waning days of the Soviet Union, the T-64 "premium" tank series represented a significant departure from the old, simple Soviet designs with its turbine engine, low weight, composite armor, and large 125-mm main gun. The design proved to be an overreach for Soviet technology, with an engine sufficiently unreliable that it was issued only to units based close to the factories.

Following the collapse and dismemberment of the Soviet Union in late 1991, the Russian state found itself faced with separatist movements in several of its remaining components, most notably Chechnya. The T-80 was by that time Russia's new premium tank, belatedly entering service in 1976. Capable of launching the Kobra antitank missile, the final production version, the T-80BV, incorporated advanced Kontact-1 ERA. The gas turbine engine proved so fuel-inefficient that it was replaced by a diesel in the final production T-80UD. The first "combat" use of the TU-80UD came in shelling the Russian Parliament building during the constitutional crisis in October 1993.

In December 1994 Chechnya declared itself independent. In a badly planned New Year's Eve surprise offensive, Russia invaded to reassert its control. The Russian commanders expected to motor into the capitol city in a show of force. Russian forces retained the old Soviet armor-heavy doctrine, and the initial incursion into the city of Grozny was a humiliating disaster. With insufficient infantry support, Russian armor rolled confidently into the city. Infantry tended to stay inside their armored fighting vehicles, commanders quickly became lost in the urban maze, and sometimes fired on each other. Russian personnel carriers were deathtraps, and tanks were prey to Chechen tank-killer teams armed only with RPGs. The tank-killers quickly learned to take advantage of the Russian tanks' limited main gun elevation, unable to fire into upper floors or basements at relatively close ranges. The T-80 proved even more vulnerable than the T-72; combustible-case main gun rounds were stored vertically along the hull sides, and protected mainly by the road wheels. Ambushers learned to fire into the thinly armored hull sides above the road wheels, setting off catastrophic explosions.

Sixty hours of close-quarter fighting destroyed the Russian Maikop Brigade. Russian sources have never owned up to their losses. An American analysis of the fighting concluded that:

> Chechens weren't afraid of tanks and BMPs. They assigned groups of RPG gunners to fire volleys at the lead and trail vehicles. Once they were destroyed, the others were picked off one-by-one. The Russian forces lost 20 of 26 tanks [other sources estimate 67 tanks], 102 of 120 BMPs, and 6 of 6 ZSU-23s in the first three days fighting …

Russia finally crushed the Chechens in a prolonged siege that pounded the city into rubble. The city would change hands twice more (August 1996, January 2000), but the burden of fighting would be borne by infantry, with massive numbers, careful reconnaissance, and specialized urban combat vehicles like the TOS-1 long-range flamethrower tank built on a T-72 chassis. This time "… armored vehicles, except on rare occasion, were kept out of the city fight. Instead, tanks and artillery were positioned on the side of hills overlooking and surrounding Grozny, and these pieces fired into the city."

In fighting outside the city old T-62s and modern T-72s saw use in ones and twos supporting infantry. The T-72 proved prone to malfunctions of the automatic loader. The Chechens quickly caught on that after each round the gun returned to the load position, offering a brief safe interval for attacking the tank.

No matter how much it was improved, the T-80 was destined to be overshadowed by its second-line stablemate, the T-72. The Russians ceased production, and the T-80 saw no further combat use. Even before the Soviet collapse, the T-72 saw widespread use in the Iran–Iraq War, by Syria in Lebanon, the Sri Lankan Civil War, the Armenia–Azerbaijan War, the Sierra Leone Civil War, the Georgian Civil War, and by the Iraqis in Kuwait. The collapse of the Soviet Union triggered various independence movements, but the most complex and violent was the disintegration of the former Yugoslavia, triggered by the secession of Slovenia. In the nasty civil warfare that ensued various nationalistic factions used tanks dating back as far as World War II (American M4s and M36 tank destroyers), T-55s and M47s, all the way to brand-new Yugoslav M-84s (license-built T-72s). In NATO peacekeeping operations various countries, including Germany and the Netherlands, used small detachments of Leopard 2A4s and 2A5s. The Bosnia peacekeeping force included American M1A1s, Leopards, and British Challenger 1 and 2 tanks. Forces in Kosovo have included, in addition, French Leclercs. A serious limitation on any extensive operations was the limited load capacity of bridges, too weak to allow significant mobility.

## CHAPTER 5

# WARS OF THE REGIONAL POWERS

*The British Empire passed quickly and with less humiliation than its French and Dutch counterparts, but decades later, the vicious politics of partition still seems to define India and Pakistan.*

Pankaj Mishra

Many feuds pre-dating the colonial era came to a boil after independence. Regional rivalries like China–Vietnam, India–Pakistan and Iran–Iraq, erupted into full-scale warfare, while other rivalries erupted into smaller-scale wars. What all had in common is that as a result of alignments with two competing powers—the Soviet Union and Communist China—and limited access by Western news media or intelligence agencies, the details of these wars remain murky. In general, however, the participants were influenced only to a limited degree by tactical practices of their patron states, with little impact upon local doctrine (if any existed at all).

## The Indo-Pakistani Wars

Tensions had simmered between the two regional powers since the partition of 1947, and much of the conflict centered (and still does) over control of Kashmir. India's difficulties in the Sino-Indian War of 1962 suggested to Pakistani leaders that the time was ripe to seize Kashmir and other disputed territories. In 1965 Pakistan infiltrated commandoes into India, and the ensuing conflict escalated into full-blown war that witnessed some of the largest armored clashes since World War II. This was not one of the usual proxy wars, since both regional powers were then Western-oriented. Both sides have remained secretive about military operations, and the details of the war remain obscure. The following numbers should not be taken as definitive.

Both armies were attempting to modernize their tank fleets, using a mishmash of old and new equipment. India had only the First (Black Elephant) Armored Division of six regiments, two equipped with Centurion Mark VII tanks. The Second Independent Armored Brigade had three regiments, one equipped with Centurions. The remaining eight independent cavalry regiments were equipped with older tanks. In all, India fielded about 185 Centurions, 350 older American M4s, many of which had been upgraded with more powerful American and French guns, 90 French AMX-13 light tanks, and an equal number of Soviet PT-76 amphibious tanks.

Pakistan had 15 cavalry regiments, most as part of the First and Sixth Armored Divisions. The Pakistani armored force was both larger and more modern, with only 300 M4s, 350 newer M47 and M48 main battle tanks, 90 M24 Chaffee light tanks suitable only for reconnaissance, and a few M36B1 tank destroyers.

On September 6, India crossed into a buffer zone, and the war began. The first use of armor came in the Indian thrust against Lahore by the 1st Infantry Division supported by three tank regiments of the 2nd Independent Armored Brigade. This thrust was blocked by Pakistani destruction of bridges over the Ichthogil Canal. Pakistani forces quickly retaliated with an armored and infantry attack on the Indian 15th Infantry Division, driving it back. The war escalated into a series of attacks and counterattacks. At Chawinda the Indian First Armored

Division was badly mauled, losing over 100 tanks. By September 10, Pakistan's First Armored Division was savaged by the Indian Fourth Mountain Division supported by tanks in the battle of Asai Uttar. The Pakistani force lost 97 tanks, the Indians 32. The war degenerated into a costly stalemate.

The war revealed major Pakistani problems, particularly poor leadership. The Pakistani military still succeeded in fighting India to a stalemate, although India is considered by most to be the "winner" of this inconclusive war.

In a purely military sense the war drove Western analysts toward erroneous conclusions. Indian tank losses were estimated at 128–200 tanks, Pakistani losses at 200 to as high as 500. No unbiased estimates exist but this perceived loss ratio, and ultimate Indian tactical successes, led many to conclude that the older Centurion was superior to the American M48. Such conclusions failed to take into account at least marginally greater Indian tactical prowess, particularly given the Pakistani penchant for armored frontal attacks on prepared position, and possibly poor maintenance.

The war also resulted in a major geopolitical shift in southern Asia. America and Britain placed an arms embargo on both sides, both took affront, and the competing Communist powers seized the advantage. The Soviet Union became the primary supplier of military aid to India, with Communist China backing Pakistan. The war accelerated development of an indigenous Indian tank manufacturing program. The British Vickers Mark I derived Vijayanta MBT entered service in 1965.

In the 1971 war, armor played a significantly lesser role. The proximal cause of the war, a separatist movement in East Pakistan (modern Bangladesh) resulted in powerful Indian intervention in which armor played a supporting role for nine infantry divisions. On December 3 Pakistan launched attacks along the border with India. In response a major Indian strategic goal was to eliminate the Pakistani Shakar Garh border salient. An Indian offensive led to a clash between Indian Centurions and Pakistani M48s southwest of Chhamb (Kashmir) in which both sides fought to a draw. On the northern margin of the salient the significant battle of Basantar/Shakargarh (December 4–11) involved only a single troop (company) of Indian tanks equipped to sweep mines. The fighting quickly bogged down in the massive Pakistani minefields. Conflict persisted, with continuing fighting that again erupted into the 1999 Kargil War.

India also purchased Soviet designs like the T-72BU/T-90. Pakistan imported the T-80UD from the Ukraine, and developed its own tanks, the al-Khalid series based on the Chinese MBT-2000. With continued development of an Indian arms industry, the Arjun entered general service in 2004, and new designs continue. Arjun is comparable in performance to most third-generation MBTs, but uses a locally developed rifled 120-mm main gun with a locally designed APFDS as its primary round.

# The Sino-Vietnamese War

Centuries of conflicts with China are one of the cornerstones of Vietnamese history. China and Vietnam had fallen at odds with each other because of increasing Soviet influence in Vietnam, and the Vietnamese incursion into Cambodia. On February 17, 1979 China invaded Vietnam.

The war saw massive use of infantry, but the Chinese deployed the Kunming Independent Tank Regiment in the initial invasion, with about 200 Type 59, Type 62, and Type 63 tanks. The Vietnamese response was swift and more effective than the Chinese expected, but the only armored force resisting the Chinese was some aged T-34/85s. In the fighting around the town of Lang Son no Vietnamese tanks directly engaged Chinese Type 62 tanks, but the offensive ground to a halt through Chinese ineptitude.

On March 6 China announced its goal—the relief of Cambodian forces—achieved, and broke off fighting. The war resulted in minor changes to the national border, but more importantly demonstrated Soviet impotence in supporting its client state, Vietnam.

## The Iran–Iraq War

On September 22, 1980, Iraq invaded Iran, spearheaded by powerful armored forces, ostensibly over control of the Shat-al-Arab waterway, a major petroleum shipping route. Iranian command functions were disorganized by the chaos of the 1978–79 revolution, but the first real Iranian resistance crystallized around Khoramshahr; about 500 Iraqi tanks led the attack on the city. By September 30, tanks of the Iraqi 3rd Armored Division managed to push into the city, but fell back after encountering Iranian Chieftain tanks and heavy infantry resistance. After two weeks of shelling, the Iraqis again attacked, and fighting continued until November 10. Iraqi tanks were unable to negotiate the narrow streets of the old city.

The decisive armored battle was Operation *Nasr* (January 5–9, 1981). Three Iranian armored regiments equipped with M60 and British Chieftain tanks advanced with inadequate infantry or air support. The Iraqis fell back upon their most favored tactic, feigning withdrawal but forming a huge three-sided box

The brief 1982 **Falklands War** between Argentina and the United Kingdom highlighted the need for more strategically mobile light armored vehicles. The British were faced with the need for infantry support vehicles, and a counter to a dozen French-made Panhard armored cars. At the end of a a 13,000–km transport path, the British deployed only eight armored vehicles, four Scimitar, and four Scorpion Armored Reconnaissance Vehicles.

into which the Iranians advanced. The sides of the box included three regiments equipped with T-62 tanks, entirely adequate to a defensive battle, but often dug in as pillboxes. Inside this kill box about 300 Iranian tanks were limited to a few roads, or floundered in deep mud, often immobilized for lack of fuel and ammunition that could not be moved forward.

Iraqi tanks and attack helicopters took a heavy toll, but the Iranians stubbornly persisted, with heavy losses. By January 8, the attacking force was spent, the single surviving regiment forced back. The Iranians had lost an estimated 215 tanks, about a quarter of their serviceable tank forces, as opposed to 45 Iraqi tanks lost. Many of the Iranian tanks were captured intact. In the end the Iraqis could not exploit the victory because of the same mobility problems that had hindered the Iranians. Both sides rapidly bled their armored forces into near collapse. The savage war of attrition continued until August 1988.

# CHAPTER 6

▓▓▓▓▓▓▓▓▓▓▓▓▓▓▓▓▓▓▓▓▓▓▓▓▓▓▓▓▓▓▓▓▓▓▓▓▓▓▓▓▓▓▓▓▓▓
▓▓▓▓▓▓▓▓▓▓▓▓▓▓▓▓▓▓▓▓▓▓▓▓▓▓▓▓▓▓▓▓▓▓▓▓▓▓▓▓▓▓▓▓▓▓

# THE ARAB–ISRAELI WARS

*The man in the tank will prevail.*

IDF Armored Corps motto

FOLLOWING WORLD WAR II THE OPPOSING Arab and Israeli armies were among the primary practitioners of armored warfare, largely because the terrain and conditions were so suitable. Long before the partition of Palestine, Israeli agents began the covert purchase of heavy weapons including ten old French R39 light tanks. The newly created Arab states were arming themselves with whatever surplus weapons could be procured on the black market or were abandoned in place by the colonial powers. Egypt had a mixed bag of American M4s and M22 Locust light tanks, British Crusaders and Matildas, and even 1930s vintage British Mark VI light tanks. The Syrians had French H35 and H39 tanks. The Lebanese were stuck with venerable French FTs. Tanks played little role in the 1948–49 War of Independence.

Eager to gain a foothold in the Mediterranean, the Soviet Union cultivated relations with Egypt, and supplied about 230 T-34/85 and IS-3M tanks, seriously skewing the balance of power. By 1955, France was selling weapons to Israel, including M4s and later AMX13 light tanks.

In November 1956, Egyptian dictator Gamal Abdel Nasser decided to restrict access to the Suez Canal. French and British petroleum tankers were the most affected, prompting both nations to intervene militarily. On November 6, a squadron of AMX-13s from the 2e Régiment Étranger de Cavalerie disembarked at Port Fouad and Port Saïd to reinforce airborne forces.

Israel invaded the Sinai peninsula in an operation heavily influenced by the old *blitzkrieg* model. The attack came as a complete surprise, advancing into the Sinai. As the major powers increasingly aligned themselves with local powers, the stage was set for a confrontation between the equipment if not the armored doctrines of the United States and the Soviet Union.

With Russia threatening direct military support to the Egyptians and the Americans condemning the "expedition," the Franco-British troops were forced to withdraw, ending the shortest war in history. In this short and undeclared war the AMX13 was unable to test its full potential. A pattern had been set for heavy Israeli reliance upon armored and airborne forces.

By 1967 both sides were armed to the teeth as part of a sort of proxy war. Egypt, Syria, and Iraq were equipped with a mix of Soviet T-34/85, T-54, T-55, and PT-76 tanks, the newest Soviet T-62s, and self-propelled guns. The Jordanian Army was equipped with American M47, M48, and M48A1 tanks. Israel was far better equipped, with about 250 American-built M48 and M48A1 tanks, many upgraded with the 105-mm L7 main gun used in the Centurion. The Israelis had also upgraded many old M4 tanks to their M50 and M51 "Super Shermans," with a 105-mm main gun. AMX13s and Centurions remained part of the mix.

Israel Tal had served in the Jewish Brigade of the British Army in World War II, and as a junior officer in the War of Independence. In 1964 Tal assumed command of Israeli armored forces, and set about making it into the centerpiece of the Israeli Defense Forces (IDF). His doctrine was based upon a triad of mobility, relentless attacks, and exploiting the greater striking range of Western-supplied tanks.

Tal's armor-heavy doctrine, with emphasis on preservation of Israel's limited military manpower, held considerable appeal to Israel's politicians. As a practical matter, Tal's doctrine would of necessity be aggressive yet strictly tactical in scope, and this led Israel into a strategic trap. Tactical success led to conquest of additional territory that Israel would never be able to completely control, and consumed manpower to defend successively extended borders. The result was a war of low-intensity attrition that continues to the present day.

Egyptian and Syrian armor doctrine imitated that of the Soviets: overwhelming numbers and acceptance of massive losses in pursuit of a clear strategic goal, the elimination of Israel. Tactically, tank crews were trained to advance in a rapid rush to within about a half-kilometer of the enemy before opening fire. This granted Israeli tank gunners, trained to fight at ranges up to 1,500 meters, an enormous advantage in a defensive battle.

Tal was a primary architect of the surprise attack known as the 1967 Six Day War. On the main southern front the Israelis massed six armored, three parachute, one infantry and one mechanized infantry brigades, to face four armored, two infantry, and one mechanized infantry divisions of the Egyptian Army. In all, the Israelis deployed about 70,000 men and 700 tanks, the Egyptians about 900 tanks and 100,000 men. In the critical battle of Abu-Ageila the Israeli 38th Armored Division with about 150 AMX13s, M50s, and Centurions outnumbered and outmatched the Egyptian 2nd Infantry Division supported by only 90 old T-34/85 tanks and 20 SU-100 tank destroyers.

Israel made extensive use of the AMX13. Casualties among crews were high, but the front-mounted engine augmented crew protection, and probably influenced later Israeli tank design. In the north the Israelis faced a smaller Syrian force, and the fighting in the Golan Heights was at shorter ranges that favored the defenders. Here Israeli airpower proved the decisive factor.

In the center the Jordanian Arab Legion took the offensive with American M47 and M48 tanks concentrated between the Jordan River and partitioned Jerusalem. The Israelis launched a counteroffensive that encircled and captured Jerusalem. Among the booty were M47 tanks that the Israelis considered obsolete, and about 100 of Jordan's M48 and M48A1 tanks that the Israelis happily absorbed into their own army.

The rapid Israeli victory captured the attention of the world, but the ineptitude of their opponents disguised the fact that the IDF was making the same mistakes as many victorious armies. The quick and easy victories led their military to shift too much emphasis onto the tank forces at the expense of infantry.

The victory had gained Israel a broad swath of useless desert, but the only real gain was that Jordan would no longer actively engage Israeli forces. Victory in fact left Israel in a more precarious position, facing Egyptian forces along the 150-km length of the Suez Canal in the 1967–70 War of Attrition, the type of struggle to which Israeli forces were least suited.

In 1968–69 Israel built the Bar Lev Line, a chain of fixed defenses along the Suez Canal. Behind it lay an elaborate road network to allow an armored division with over 300 tanks and an infantry force to deploy, and slow Egyptian penetration until a general mobilization could be effected. Generals Ariel Sharon and Israel Tal objected to a fixed defense, since static positions could be pre-targeted.

In 1970 the Israeli government decided that overseas armaments supplies might be slow in coming or uncertain in future wars, so the country needed an indigenous tank industry. By 1973 Tal was the team leader in the development of a tank design that became the Merkava (Chariot).

## The Yom Kippur War

In this general offensive by Arab forces the strategically decisive foe would be Egypt. While the Israeli government mulled over a preemptive attack, on October 6, 1973, the Egyptians breached the berms of the Bar Lev Line in less than three hours, using high-pressure pumps mounted on barges to wash away the loose sand of the berm. The strongpoints were inundated by artillery and air attack. Israel had only one armored brigade forward deployed, and piecemeal counterattacks had little effect. Once through the Bar Lev Line the Egyptians advanced quickly into the Sinai. On October 8, the Israelis were finally able to organize a major counterattack to relieve units holding out across the canal from the city of al-Ismailya, only to be driven back with heavy losses to new Soviet 9M14 Malyutka (NATO "Sagger") antitank missiles and RPGs.

The use of Soviet antitank missiles exposed the weakness of Israel's excessive reliance upon armored forces, and brought their military close to disaster. The offensively oriented armored force was unable to cope with a massive infantry onslaught, and tank losses were heavy until the Egyptian offensive stumbled to a halt in part because of logistics, in part because of Egyptian reluctance to move beyond the protection of their heavy surface-to-air missile batteries. This respite and a massive American airlift of more modern weapons like the M60 tank staved off disaster for Israel.

On the northern front Syrian forces made significant gains, but an Israeli counteroffensive soon threatened Damascus. In a series of small battles both sides fought to near total exhaustion; the Israeli 7th Armored Brigade was reduced to six tanks. When the Israeli brigade was reinforced by 15 tanks, the debilitated Syrian forces were forced into retreat. In an effort to reduce pressure on Syria, the Egyptians resumed their stalled offensive.

With American weapon resupply assured, Israel shifted back to a familiar offensive posture. On October 15, the spearhead of an Israeli counterattack by two armored divisions crossed the canal, and ran amok among the undefended missile batteries and logistical units in the sort of battle that Israeli doctrine dreamt of but seldom achieved. By October 24 the Israelis had surrounded Suez City and the Egyptian Third Army, but Egyptian air and artillery attacks on the pontoon bridges limited Israeli resupply to a trickle.

Increasing tensions between the Americans and Soviets threatened a widening of the war and the patrons forced a cease-fire that left the two sides intermingled across a huge battle area and virtually assured local resumptions of fighting. Israel Tal—now commander of all ground forces on the southern front—was ordered to resume the attack, but refused the order as unethical, ending his command career in all but name.

As part of the Camp David Accords Israel returned most of the Sinai to Egyptian control and withdrew from around Suez City.

One of the lessons of the war was that excessive Israeli reliance upon armor, small elite infantry forces, and offensive action had left the IDF ill-prepared to repulse major infantry attacks. A more balanced force with a larger infantry component would prove crucial in the ongoing struggles with Palestinian irregular forces.

## Enter the Chariot

The new Merkava did not enter service until 1978, after the primary need for it had passed into history. The design philosophy emphasized crew survivability, quick repair of battle damage using modular armor, high-speed mobility, and relatively low cost. The low turret profile was reduced to move the three-man turret crew into the heavily armored hull. The engine was placed in front to move vulnerable crew spaces behind the mass of the engine and transmission. A sizeable tunnel under the rear deck connected the crew space to a large rear escape hatch. This feature led many to erroneously assume that the tank was designed to double as an infantry transport. In fact it was sometimes used to evacuate wounded, as a cramped command post, and occasionally to transport up to six infantrymen. The main armament was a 120-mm smoothbore gun capable of firing the LAHAT antitank missile.

Like most vehicles the Merkava went through multiple design changes, culminating in the 2004 Mark IV, with improved armor including mine-resistant belly armor, improved ammunition stowage, a new 120-mm gun with a revolving magazine, and the ELBIT communications/battle management system that incorporates intelligence from other vehicles, surveillance drones, and other sources and distributes it at unit level.

The Mark IVm "Wind Coat" incorporates the TROPHY active antimissile defense system that uses radar to detect an incoming

*The Israeli Merkava places considerable emphasis on crew survivability. The vertical turret sides indicate that this is a Merkava I. (Cansière)*

missile, evaluate its potential threat level, intercepts it with a shotgun-like munition if necessary, and advise the crew of the source of the enemy fire. The primary disadvantage of the system is cost, and the danger to nearby infantry, a serious disadvantage in urban or close-quarter combat. Thus far the system has conclusively proven effective only against longer-range or single-missile attacks.

# The Palestinian Resistance

With Jordan and Egypt neutralized, Israel's struggles with its neighbors quickly transitioned to a counterinsurgency to which its armor-heavy forces were ill-suited. The center of Palestinian resistance shifted to Lebanon, whose central government had disintegrated in a protracted civil war between 1975 and 1990.

In response to cross-border provocations, Israel briefly invaded southern Lebanon in 1978, and again occupied the region from mid-1982 until January 1985. Both incursions were disastrous for the civilian population, and no lasting results were accomplished. Palestinian resistance in southern Lebanon, the West Bank, and Gaza grew inexorably. Increasing Iranian influence over the local Hezbollah has marked the protracted violence of the Israeli–Palestinian struggle.

In another controversial July–August 2006 incursion against Hezbollah forces in southern Lebanon, Israel used about 400 of the various models of the Merkava, including the Mark IV. Hezbollah was lavishly equipped with antitank missiles, and the Hezbollah fighters used tactics in which teams attacked from several quarters and struck the more vulnerable sides and rear of tanks. Losses among the tank corps proved particularly controversial. It is hard to sort fact from propaganda on both sides, and IDF sources typically report only vehicles irreparably destroyed as losses. Corporal Michael Mizrahi described the missile strike that wrecked his tank as "a boom, flames, and smoke," but the protected ammunition stowage and a sophisticated fire suppression system saved crewmen like him from more serious burns. The Merkava's vulnerability to missiles proved limited, but about 10 percent were seriously damaged as the tanks proved to be highly symbolic targets.

More effective were large IEDs, which totally destroyed two tanks; the IED threat forced the Israelis to adopt a tactic of sending an armored bulldozer to clear a movement path through high-risk areas. Familiar complaints were that tanks were used in small groups, with inadequate infantry support. Israeli public opinion was soured by the cost of the tank versus the failure of its vaunted invulnerability, and the incursion was considered a failure, particularly among those opposing the war.

In the asymmetric warfare in the Occupied Territories, Israeli armor does not always have things its own way. In Gaza on February 2012, a Merkava III was struck by a large IED, toppling the tank onto its side, blowing off the turret, and killing three crew members. An American assessment of Hamas insurgents in the 2012 "Gaza War" concluded that although no Israeli tanks were lost, Hamas antitank tactics were becoming increasingly sophisticated, and that Israeli response was marred by overwhelming and often indiscriminate firepower in the densely populated area.

# CHAPTER 7

# A NEW ORDER IN THE MIDDLE EAST AND BEYOND

*You can feel a tank coming down the street, you can feel the street rumbling.*

Lieutenant Colonel Bart Sloat, U.S.M.C.

IN THE VOLATILE MIDDLE EAST MANY oil-rich nations acquired tanks, as symbols of military power, with no clear doctrine on how to utilize them. The two primary powers contending for dominance were Iraq and Iran, and with Iran debilitated by revolution and war, Iraq was clearly the dominant power. Saddam Hussein chafed at what they believed to be the heavy price paid by Iraq, on behalf of other Arab countries, in the war with Iran, exacerbated by a dispute with Kuwait over production of an oil field that straddled the border. In early August 1990, Iraq conquered Kuwait in a three-day war, with massive armored forces brushing aside the tiny Kuwaiti army equipped with 15 Yugoslavian M-84 MBTs and 143 Chieftains. On August 2, the Kuwaiti 35th Armored Brigade fought a rearguard action, the battle of Jal al Atraf, against two Iraqi Republican Guard mechanized divisions. The Kuwaitis acquitted themselves well, but were forced to withdraw into Saudi Arabia when their ammunition was depleted. In some ways the brief battle was a portent of things to come, as the elite Republican Guard was, in this action, remarkable mainly for its blundering.

## Operation *Desert Storm*

American forces comprised by far the largest contingent of the Coalition force assembled to expel Iraq from Kuwait, but the war caught America in transition between the Marine Corps M60A1 RISE and the Army M60A3, and the new M1A1 MBT for both services.

The first tactical problem was breaching the Iraqi defenses, which were patterned after those that had proven successful in the war with Iran. The Iraqis constructed deep minefields and wire barriers, and segmented the battle space into boxes, compartments defined by obstacles and minefields that in some way duplicated the World War II *bocage*. But the Iraqis were lackadaisical about maintenance, and in some cases wind had unearthed mines. Armored vehicles were emplaced as fixed positions (some were actually partially buried, incapable of movement). Iraqi Army conscripts formed the front-line units, with Republican Guard forces as a reserve—and to destroy any Iraqi Army units that tried to retreat.

*Desert Storm* saw the application of another old-yet-new-again concept. The doctrine of rapid dominance (popularly known as **"shock and awe"**) was based upon the use of combined arms in overwhelming and spectacular—but specifically targeted—violence to psychologically paralyze the enemy. It was a doctrine ideally suited to the relatively open desert.

The *Desert Storm* operational plan assigned units to specific tasks on the basis of perceived abilities. Two American Marine Corps divisions—with more infantry dismounts, bridging assets to cross water barriers, and amphibious personnel carriers—reinforced by the tanks of the Army's Tiger Brigade and Arab Coalition forces would launch a frontal attack northward along the more densely settled coastal strip. A Marine Expeditionary Brigade stood offshore, preventing the Iraqis from redeploying coastal defense troops.

Further inland American Army and British mechanized forces would maneuver across the open desert into southern Iraq, then turn east to envelop Kuwait City from the west. On the far western flank American and French light infantry forces would sweep into Iraq to sever the Kuwait City–Baghdad highway.

A fundamental change in doctrine was prioritization of targets. The Coalition would depend heavily upon airpower, so highest priority would be to destroy Iraqi air defense weapons. The highest priority targets would be Soviet ZSU-23/4s, four radar-directed 23-mm rapid-firing cannons on a tank chassis that posed a threat to low-flying airplanes or helicopters.

A primary task was to breach the Iraqi minefields, but the technology had advanced far beyond "Hobart's Funnies." The main breaching operations would be in the zone of the Marines and the Army Tiger Brigade. Some of the equipment—mine plows, rollers, and dozer blades—would be mounted on tanks, to be discarded after the breach was achieved to free the tank for fighting.

After a massive aerial onslaught that paralyzed Iraqi command and control functions, breaching operations and a massive ground assault began. The result was foreordained. Most Iraqi resistance just crumbled. Company Executive Officer Chris Freitus noted that in infantry defenses "Heads bobbed up and down, looking much like a prairie dog town."

When the Iraqi T-72—the most modern tank in their inventory—was struck the stored combustible-case ammunition detonated, blowing the turret as high as 10 meters into the air and incinerating the crew. The Russian doctrine of massive numbers of expendable tanks (and crews) proved less than appealing to the Iraqis, many of whom simply abandoned their tanks and ran for it.

The Iraqi armored units that fought blundered about, unaware of the tactical situation. In the Reveille Battle the Iraqi 8th Mechanized Brigade crossed a raised road berm in columns, only to be picked off by M1A1s of C Company, 4th Marine Tank Battalion. In seven minutes the Americans destroyed 30 T-72s, four T-55s, and seven personnel carriers without loss.

The largest armored clash was the battle of 73 Easting (named for a map longitude line) when Iraqi armor of the 18th Mechanized Brigade, Tawakalna Division and the 9th Armored Brigade/12th Armored Divisions attacked elements of the American 2nd Armored Cavalry Regiment. In this action the Iraqis fought with atypical tenacity and mechanized infantry coordinated well with tanks. But American tanks completely outclassed Iraqi T-55, T-62, and T-72 tanks. Iraqi losses in the one-sided battle and American counterattacks are hard to assess, but the American force (nine M1A1 tanks and supporting Bradley Fighting Vehicles) destroyed at least 85 tanks (some sources say 160), 260 other vehicles, and killed or captured some 2,300 Iraqis.

The AMX-30 saw combat with both French and Qatari forces, and were credited the destruction of several Iraqi T-55s tanks. The Iraqis quickly withdrew the vaunted T-72s from the path of the British Challenger 1 tanks of the 1st Armoured Division, but nevertheless one Challenger achieved the longest-range tank kill of the war, at a range of 5 kilometers.

The war proved that the huge Iraqi army was a paper tiger, with no clear doctrine or even an understanding of fundamental tactics.

# Operation *Iraqi Freedom*

Controversial from its inception, the second war with Iraq was nominally fought in reaction to the major terrorist attacks upon the United States in September 2001. This time there were no clear and limited goals, only a nebulous plan to overthrow the Saddam Hussein regime and rebuild the politics of the Middle East. The strategic plan was an extension of the *Desert Storm* plan: overwhelming destruction of Iraqi military power and this time occupation of Iraq.

The major part of the strategic plan revolved around rapid thrusts by mechanized columns, and was in many ways a replay of the prior war. U.S. Army mechanized forces would sweep through the open desert to the west, the Marine Corps with their infantry-heavy forces would sweep up the more densely populated Tigris–Euphrates Valley. The British 1st Armoured Division would secure the crucial petroleum-loading facilities at Basra to prevent the environmental mayhem of the last war.

The bulk of Iraqi resistance was expected to face the Marines, and would test their doctrine of "combined-arms effect," the selective use of overwhelming but carefully targeted violence. The doctrinal goal was to paralyze the enemy, to present him with simultaneous and parallel attacks, keep him off balance, and present him with a torrent of irresolvable dilemmas.

The Iraqi border defenses were farcical, and again the Iraqi military largely disintegrated in the face of the Coalition onslaught. Captain Brian R. Lewis observed that again "I saw a T-55 not 15 meters to my flank. It was completely dug in with burlap camouflage and it was dug in to the point of not being able to engage with its main gun." Effective resistance came largely as ambushes by the predominantly non-Iraqi *fedayeen* volunteers as armored task forces moved through towns and villages.

The capture of Basra saw the combat debut of the Challenger 2 as they clashed with ambushers and outclassed Iraqi T-55s. One tank was struck by a Milan missile and 14 RPGs, but the crew remained unscathed; another was reportedly struck by 70 RPGs. The only Challenger destroyed was lost to a friendly fire incident on March 25.

As the British tightened the noose around Basra, on March 25 a large column of Iraqi armor broke out of the city, inexplicably headed southeast. One group of 14 T-55s clashed with Challengers and was annihilated.

American forces were able to quickly sweep into the Iraqi capital Baghdad, hampered more by logistical problems than enemy action. But there emerged doctrinal problems that would bedevil the next phase of the war.

An unfortunate corollary to the widely known "shock and awe" doctrine is what the military calls collateral damage: near total destruction of civilian infrastructure like water and electrical supplies, too often with heavy civilian casualties. One manifestation of the doctrine was the U.S. Army's "thunder runs" through Baghdad. Executed by divisions that had powerful mechanized units but relatively few infantry dismounts for urban combat, armored columns raced through populated areas shooting up everything in sight. These were repeated incursions with no intent to clear or occupy the areas attacked. The idea was simply to slice apart potential centers of resistance, demoralize the enemy, and "keep his head down." Civilians inevitably became casualties, fueling the insurgency that the Multi-National Force (MNF) had hoped to avoid. The insurgency and later civil war along ethnic lines commenced almost immediately, and over the next eight years would tax the MNF.

At the other end of the spectrum, the British—based on their long experience in counterinsurgency warfare—proposed to counter the insurgency with a law-and-order approach: building relationships with the locals who would then rat out any local insurgents. Tanks played a supportive role in this doctrine, but unfortunately the Challenger 2 had acquired a reputation as impregnable in the eyes of the British public. In August 2006 an RPG-29 with a tandem warhead struck the underside of a tank, severely wounding the driver. The incident was not publicized until nine months later, leading to charges of a cover-up. In 2007 another was damaged and a crewman wounded by an IED.

With its own experience of counterinsurgency warfare, the U.S. Marine Corps doctrine was in the middle. The idea was to employ a "spreading ink blot" strategy, to occupy critical locations inside the urban areas, destroy insurgents who were drawn to attack these centers, then spread out to capture and control progressively larger areas.

Tank urban warfare doctrine would play a signal role in all these strategies, evolving as the insurgency grew in scope and violence. The political and military complexities of the insurgency could (and would) fill many books, but the bottom line is that tank doctrine returned to its infantry-support roots. Tank unit officers searched every available reference, particularly to the prolonged fighting in Hue City in 1968.

After Vietnam the U.S. Army had concentrated on a potential war in Europe, and one corollary to that general doctrine was to avoid urban combat: cities were seen as traps that absorbed strength and time. But as Army Lieutenant Colonel Ralph Peters had pointed out in his 1996 essay *Our Soldiers, Their Cities*, increasing global urbanization made cities the battlefields of the future. Faced with an urban insurgency, the Army quickly refined its counterinsurgency tank doctrine. In the 2004 offensive to recapture Fallujah, tank cannons were routinely used to blast gaping holes in buildings, with considerable collateral damage. By 2005, the 3rd Armored Cavalry in Tal Afar was applying a doctrine that emphasized more discriminating use of firepower,

The **tandem warhead** is designed to counter ERA. A first charge detonates the explosive armor block, and the second shaped charge attacks the same spot, penetrating the armor.

and the intimidation power of tanks, to minimize civilian casualties and destruction of infrastructure.

The British and the U.S. Marine Corps had, by the nature of their mission roles, maintained some expertise in urban warfare. Infantry commanders reported that heavy armor could often end fighting just by its arrival. As Lieutenant Colonel Bart Sloat (U.S.M.C. infantry) observed, "You can feel a tank coming down the street, you can feel the street rumbling. In An Najaf, that's what caused a lot of them (insurgents) to pull back." When the enemy did resist, the precision direct firepower of tanks could both minimize collateral damage, and bring firepower to bear on enemy positions in the first floors of multi-story buildings, or basement positions inaccessible to aircraft or artillery. The tanks also had significant roles to play in battlespace shaping: cordoning off cities, surveillance with their superior imaging systems, elimination of specific targets (particularly insurgent leaders located by intelligence resources), and sheer intimidation. Not all combat was urban, and tanks were also used in patrolling the countryside, and in search and destroy missions.

Public opinion in America eventually soured on the war, and President Bush signed a withdrawal status of forces agreement in 2008. The incoming Obama administration delayed the withdrawal, but by mid-December 2011 it was completed.

The American withdrawal left a void that was quickly exploited by the jihadist Islamic State of Iraq and Syria (ISIS, also known by the acronym ISIL—Islamic State of Iraq and the Levant—or its Arabic acronym Daesh), which captured several major cities by 2014. Since then the Iraqi government has been engaged in a bloody slog to recapture areas under ISIS control. The reconstituted Iraqi Army was equipped with 140 M1A1M tanks (without depleted uranium armor), used in an infantry support role. An undetermined number have been lost in action, including some reportedly captured by the insurgents. The losses are primarily to advanced antitank missiles like the Russian 9K11 Kornet.

# Yemen

Entering service too late for the first Gulf War, French Leclercs were first deployed in the Kosovo peace-keeping operation (1999) and Lebanon (2006); in the latter a platoon of Leclercs were involved in a brief standoff with a platoon of Israeli Merkavas. The Leclerc saw its first actual combat in 2015 with two United Arab Emirates battalions fighting Houthi rebels in Yemen. The Yemenis profited from the experiences of others, operating in support of infantry and in turn constantly protected by special infantry teams. Yemen, with its complex urban, harsh desert, and mountain terrains also required a rethinking of combat doctrine, with emphasis on armored raids to hold the rebels out of effective range for attacks on Coalition bases. The vehicles suffered considerably from desert conditions: rubber track blocks deteriorated, machine guns frequently jammed, and engine ventilators broke down.

IEDs and antitank mines damaged the tracks and suspension systems of three tanks, but stories differ regarding the fate of a fourth. One source claims that the tank was fired at with an RPG but additional protection by armor grills (AZUR kit) prevented the round from penetrating. Another source claims that the Leclerc was knocked out by a Russian AT-5 missile that penetrated the front of the tank, killing the driver and injuring the tank commander. The rebels more typically concentrated fire on sights and optics to blind the crews and in firing on exterior machine guns to prevent their use. They would also scramble or intercept radio communications.

The rebels used the abandoned tanks for propaganda videos and then destroyed them. Limited information suggests that the Leclercs are actually superior in crew survivability to M1A2s used by the Saudis in Yemen. Saudi Arabia has limited access to the region and been even more secretive about tank losses, but as of mid-2016 it is believed that the Saudis have lost around 20 M1A2 tanks.

# Somalia

*Desert Storm* had not absolved the U.S. Marine Corps of its expeditionary responsibilities, and in late December 1992 a platoon of five M1A1 tanks were included with the American-led peacekeeping force in Somalia. Inexplicably, again the tanks were landed without main gun ammunition, leading to perhaps the strangest tank battle in history. On January 7, 1993, four M1A1s barged into a Somali compound to confront six Somali M47s. When the Marines opened fire with .50 caliber machine guns (their heaviest weapons), the Somalis thought they were ranging guns, and abandoned their tanks. The tanks later proved useful as non-lethal measures in crowd control by moving backward to drive back crowds with the intense heat of their exhaust. When the Marines were withdrawn only Pakistani light armor remained, and some analysts believe that the absence of intimidating heavy armor helped contribute to the debacle depicted in the book and film *Black Hawk Down*.

# Afghanistan

The terrorists who had brought down the World Trade Towers had been directed from the failed state of Afghanistan, so the first American retaliation was an incursion into that land-locked country. American analysts had studied the Soviet failure, and there was a perception that there was little scope for heavy armor, and that tanks would arouse resistance since the Soviets

**Ranging guns** are small-caliber weapons that have the same ballistic characteristics as a cannon round; if the small round hits the target, the cannon round will also.

had used tanks indiscriminately to terrorize the populace. Not until December 2006 did Canada deploy a platoon of Leopard tanks to the country, followed by a Danish contingent of the Jydske Dragonregiment (Jutland Dragoons) that included three Leopard 2A5 tanks. The tanks soon proved their worth in surveillance as well as infantry support. The Danes reported that tanks actually minimized collateral damage. Direct cannon fire "reduced the need for air support. Tank fire, which is frightenly [sic] accurate, pentetrates [sic] walls but usually does not level a mud-brick compound the way large bombs dropped by aircraft can. This makes reconstruction in the area far easier once the Taliban have been removed."

On July 25, 2008, an IED inflicted the first death of a Danish Leopard 2 crewman. Eventually the U.S. Marine Corps deployed a 14-tank company of M1A2 tanks to Afghanistan, where their superior fire-control systems proved an unexpected boon. In the desert tanks could see far into the distance, and cooperated with stealthy scout-sniper teams:

> The combo allowed the Marines to both covertly observe enemy movement and call in artillery or air assets far beyond the range of their [tank] guns. Tankers and scout-snipers could covertly observe routine activities in towns and villages.

## The Syrian Civil War

In 2011, several Syrian provinces rebelled against the Assad regime as part of the "Arab Spring" movement, triggering civil war. One of the first moves of the government was to send in tanks—mainly T-72Bs—to terrorize and subdue the populace. The situation quickly became confused as foreign governments like Russia supported Assad, and a fractious rebel coalition that included nationalist groups, jihadist groups, and ISIS fought among themselves while opposing the regime. The Syrian Army deploys tanks primarily as direct infantry support vehicles, with no clear doctrine to govern their use.

Prevention of access byWestern news media and the nature of the fighting—with the main center of resistance, Aleppo, under prolonged siege—make this another opaque war. As in most recent wars, a hodgepodge of weapons made their way into rebel hands, including Russian and U.S.-made antitank missiles. As of early 2017 these and other weapons have seriously depleted the Syrian tank fleet, and as many as 1,000 may have been destroyed. Most appear to have been lost to close assault by infantry in urban fighting.

# Other Events

Turkey has long conducted a war against Kurdish separatists in its southern provinces. The Syrian civil war allowed the Kurds to gain control of large areas of remote northern Syria. In August 2016, Turkey intervened, initially sending upgraded M60s, and in December 2016 deploying its Leopard 2A4s into the Kurdish territories. By year's end at least five had been destroyed by missiles and IEDs, the heaviest loss of Leopards in any conflict (some sources assert that two were captured by ISIS and subsequently destroyed by air strikes).

The end of the Cold War, and particularly the elimination of Soviet hegemony, triggered a number of smaller conflicts in Eastern Europe, and other conflicts sprang up in various quarters of the world. These included but are not limited to the Nagorno-Karabakh War (Armenia versus Azerbaijan), the Tajikistan Civil War, the Algerian Civil War, the Rwandan Civil War, the South Ossetian War (Georgia and Russian intervention), the Libyan Civil War, the Syrian Civil War, the South Sudanese Conflict, the Ukraine (Russian intervention), the Nigerian Boko-Haram guerrilla war, and a second round of Nagorno-Karabakh clashes.

▓▓▓▓▓▓▓▓▓▓▓▓▓▓▓▓▓▓▓▓▓▓▓▓▓▓▓▓▓▓▓▓▓▓▓▓▓▓▓▓▓▓▓▓
▓▓▓▓▓▓▓▓▓▓▓▓▓▓▓▓▓▓▓▓▓▓▓▓▓▓▓▓▓▓▓▓▓▓▓▓▓▓▓▓▓▓▓▓

# CHAPTER 8

# THE PRESENT AND FUTURE OF THE TANK

*Everything is becoming science fiction. From the margins of an almost invisible literature has sprung the intact reality of the 20th century.*

J. G. Ballard

IN THE 21ST CENTURY ANY ASPIRING military power must maintain an armored force, if for no other purpose than prestige. A few maintain miniscule tank fleets to intimidate domestic political opposition (the Central African Republic, four old T-55s; Malawi, a single T-55). Even old T-34s and M4s remain in local service in places like Mali and Uruguay. Other nations are forced to build and maintain modern tank fleets because of belligerent neighbors. Most countries manage to purchase MBTs, but the overwhelming majority of these are inexpensive, easy to operate and maintain export designs like the T-72 and its derivatives such as the Polish PT16, a T-72 with additional armor and a domestically manufactured main gun. Various Chinese designs have also proven popular on the export market. Designs purposely developed for the export market, like the Brazilian Osorio have often proven to be failures or sold only in small numbers (the Austrian SK-105 Kurassier). Tanks are even used as a strange sort of international currency, like the 325 or so T-80 series tanks given to South Korea in partial payment of debts; most were sold on the secondary export market.

Numerous older American M48s and M60s remain in service, but modern Western designs like the American M1 series, British Challenger 2, and French Leclerc have met with limited success on the export market, either because of political restrictions on sales, or their cost and complexity. By far the most widely marketed Western tank is the German Leopard series, used by 19 countries.

More industrialized countries who feel themselves under threat from neighbors have developed indigenous designs, like the Argentine TAM, Indian Arjun, Iranian Zulfigar, various Japanese types, the South Korean K1 (a much-modified derivative of the American M1 prototype) and the next-generation K2 Black Panther, the Israeli Merkava, and heavily modified imports like the Pakistani al-Zarrar (Chinese Type 59) and al-Khalid (Chinese MBT-2000 variant).

Though most major powers continue to develop new designs, few reach production. The exception is Russia, which continues to field new MBTs like the T-90 and the limited-issue Armata.

At this point in time Russia and China remain in essence large but regional powers, with MBTs able to fill perceived needs. Of the major powers, America almost alone faces a major need for global mobility, thus far filled primarily by M1 series MBTs and their wheeled stable-mates, Strykers and Light Armored Vehicles (LAVs). Forward-deployed Marine Corps Battalion Landing

**Black Panther** is an excellent example of a tank designed to meet specific local conditions. Its special suspension allows it to tilt far beyond the normal range in order to traverse steep slopes and maintain a stable horizontal firing platform in Korea's rugged terrain.

Teams aboard Navy ships are often accompanied by a platoon or section of M1 tanks, and additional tanks are in permanent storage aboard maritime pre-positioning ships at various places around the globe. The concept is that personnel will be flown in to prepare and man these heavy weapons. The basic strategic model is that U.S. Marine Corps divisions (Marine Expeditionary Forces, or MEFs) and Army air-transportable light divisions must "hold the line" until heavier units can be deployed.

Despite periodic attempts at resurrection, the light tank concept remains in eclipse, its traditional reconnaissance role assumed by satellites, drones, manned aircraft, light tracked vehicles like the Russian BRM, or wheeled vehicles like the Stryker and LAV families.

The concept of a rapidly deployable light tank is a recurring theme in U.S. Army tank doctrine, like the M8 Armored Gun System (cancelled in 1997). Despite repeated failures, several countries still develop and attempt to market light tank concept vehicles like the South African Tank Technology Demonstrator (TTD). The most recent American entry is the General Dynamics "Griffin," a resurrection of an older design, unveiled in 2016. Thus far most such designs have not been widely accepted, and have failed to find significant export markets, the exceptions being the elderly PT-76 amphibious tank and its Chinese derivative, the American-built  Stingray (106 sold to Thailand), the Polish PL-01 (in the concept stage in 2017), and a few indigenous designs based on IFV hulls.

Seeming alternative designs like the American M1128 Mobile Gun System, a 105-mm cannon mounted on the Stryker wheeled combat vehicle, are dedicated infantry-support guns, and demonstrably lack the battlefield survivability of the tank.

Despite their utility, the great intangible is the future of the entire tank concept. Tanks have repeatedly been declared obsolete, as with the seeming ascendancy of the antitank gun in the 1930s, the threat from missiles beginning with the Yom Kippur War, modern attack helicopters, and dedicated tank-killing munitions like top-attack bomblets. However the reality is that the tank is the only weapons system capable of carrying a precision direct-fire infantry-support cannon around the battlefield with some assurance of survivability. For the foreseeable future this support role does not seem in danger of being usurped by either artillery or aircraft, as both remain blunt-force weapons that inflict considerable collateral damage, particularly in urban warfare.

Though it will undoubtedly survive as a weapons system, the tank's form is uncertain. Some concepts like the electromagnetic rail gun as main armament will undoubtedly fall by the wayside. Great changes are more likely to be driven by the changing nature of warfare itself, with increasing emphasis on urban combat and information systems.

Traditionally seen as traps for armored forces, cities are now regarded as the battlegrounds of the future, struggles to control populations rather than empty spaces. The nature of urban combat is evolving rapidly—as witness the addition of jamming equipment on fighting vehicles to prevent the use of cell phones as detonators for IEDs. No conceivable armor can provide adequate protection against the increasing power and sophistication of antitank missiles, and active protective systems will be an absolute requirement. "Smart" munitions will also play a role in future urban combat, particularly projectiles that can be fired over walls or through windows to detonate inside rooms and other spaces. Of course all these must be balanced against the competing need for capability to counter a potential enemy's armor.

Probably the most fundamental changes will be in electronics—surveillance, detection, communications, and management of the torrent of data coming into the tank commander's ken. The existing problem is that many current systems simply overload the commander with a massive flow of information (much of it of no immediate value) that the human brain cannot quickly process. This problem first appeared in the earliest days of armored combat, and reached numbing proportions in the invasion of Iraq.

It may well be that all these requirement will at last force the resurrection of a highly sophisticated light tank. Only time will tell.

# ACKNOWLEDGEMENTS

Unless directly quoted, the interpretations and opinions expressed herein are ours alone, and do not reflect the policies of any military or governmental agency. Photos were provided by the Association du Souvenir de Sommepy-Tahure (France), and author photos are by permission from Colonel Curnier from the Musée du Général Estienne (also known as the Saumur Tank Museum) and Aberdeen Proving Ground, Maryland. Additional period photos are from the Grey Research Center and the U.S. Marine Corps History Division, MCB Quantico; the U.S. National Archives II, College Park MD; The U.S. Library of Congress, Washington DC; and the U.S. Department of Defense and the U.S. Defense Intelligence Agency. Lieutenant Colonel Ken Estes (U.S.M.C., ret.) kindly provided additional photos from his sources. Documentary resources were provided on loan through the Katy Branch, Harris County (Texas) Public Library. The final manuscript was edited by Ruth Sheppard and Catherine Gilbert.